THE
CAPTAIN NEMO COOKBOOK PAPERS

A NAUTICAL FANTASY

CAPTAIN NEMO COOKBOOK PAPERS

EVERYONE'S GUIDE TO ZEN & THE ART OF BOATING IN HARD TIMES ILLUSTRATED

BY HAL PAINTER

INTERNATIONAL MARINE PUBLISHING COMPANY
Camden, Maine

©1986 by Hal Painter

Typeset by The Key Word, Inc., Belchertown, Massachusetts
Printed and bound by BookCrafters, Chelsea, Michigan

Published by International Marine Publishing Company
21 Elm Street, Camden, Maine 04843
(207) 236-4342

Library of Congress Cataloging-in-Publication Data

Painter, Hal.
    The Captain Nemo cookbook papers.

    1. Sailing—Anecdotes, facetiae, satire, etc.
I. Title.
PN6231.S15P3 1986   797.1'24'0207   86-7164
ISBN 0-87742-206-0

For Masako, who kept the boat on course, for Michio and Mark, a rare crew indeed, and with especial thanks to Commander Don Cochrane, for inspirational shore support all the way to Zipangu and back.

H.P., KMT
Friends of Snow Planet
Ski Touring & Small Boat
Cruising Society,
Vashon Island, 1986

CONTENTS

PART III: The Ultimate Getaway Boat

PART I

COOKING ALONG WITH CAPTAIN NEMO

Chapter *1*

Clever Fellows

Potent Quotes

"Among the rapid changes in yachting, there is now emerging a fascinating group of people who harken back to old-line tradition—the oldest of them all, survival."

Jim Brown
Trimaran Designer

"I fling aside my food-sticks and cup,
I cannot eat nor drink . . .
I pull out my dagger,
I peer four ways in vain.
But I suddenly dream of riding a boat,
sailing for the sun . . ."

Li Po's 8th century
commentary on *that*
Administration's economic
policy

OME TIME AGO, WHEN this book was in the heat of progress, it was Captain Ernie Hall who asked, "What the hell you calling this *Captain Nemo's Cookbook* for when it hasn't a damned thing to do with cooking?"

We sat on a coral beach that faced the lagoon, on the capital island of Majuro in the Marshall Island archipelago. The calendar said December, but the equatorial sun howled boiling August.

How to explain this to this crazy old coot (and I say this with as much affection as consternation) was a puzzle. When it comes to talk about boats and the boating life, Captain Ernie thinks he knows it all. I don't know, maybe he does. Still, I had to think before answering.

Captain Nemo is an invention of Jules Verne's, and it is safe to say that in the book *Twenty Thousand Leagues Under the Sea*, modern man is given his first glimpse of what would seem the ultimate getaway boat, a home-built submarine called the *Nautilus*. In it, that marvelous crank Captain Nemo is heard to cry out, with utter confidence, "Get thee to the bosom of the sea—only there is independence."

Suffice it to say at the moment that not even cannonballs fired point-blank were able to dissuade this man from giving the world quite a lesson in what it means to own one's own boat, have it paid for, and sail his way as damned well he pleases. No man has embraced the bosom of the sea in so grand a fashion.

Captain Ernie, I knew, thinks it a great idea, all this, that Jules Verne was quite a guy for his having given us such a fine example of self-sufficiency and independence. But he adds, with disarming pride, "I've been doing for years what Captain Nemo only did in a book, for chrissake—getting the hell off the land, minding my own business, and keeping to sea as best I can.

"I can't afford no submarine full of King Louis the XIV furniture and stuff, not to mention a goddamned pipe organ. My harmonica suits me just fine." The truth is, Captain Ernie can't play the harmonica, but you have to hear it to know that.

Anyway, it wasn't a pipe organ that Captain Nemo kept aboard. It was more on the order of a grand piano.

Captain Ernie can at times be cantankerous, especially when he's hungry. And perhaps it was that day that he'd been too long sitting against a palm, in the godawful heat of midday here, waiting for our mutual friend Alice to come along and announce lunch.

I heard his stomach growl as he fanned at flies with an old Panama hat just as I said the wrong thing at exactly the wrong time, which was, "There's this scene in the Jules Verne book, Captain Ernie, that has Captain Nemo telling a distinguished visitor—they're pushed back from the table, you see, after an excellent breakfast, smoking great cigars that Nemo claims to have fashioned from seaweed—and then Nemo remarks, proud as hell, 'My cook's a clever fellow.' The visitor agrees. Nemo's cook *had* to be clever fellow, he accedes, to have turned out livers of dolphin fish that were every bit as good as ragout of pork. Everything served that morning, including the anemone preserve, was prepared from odds and ends gathered from the bosom of the sea."

I was still trying to get it through his head what *my* book is all about, but the look he gave me made me feel I'd deliberately set out to try his patience. He put his hat to his face and said to me through it, "Too much poesy. You need more string-beans."

"Stringbeans?"

"I went downtown shopping yesterday, and I found this Japanese fellow who sold me a whole case of stringbeans that had got damaged. Cans were all rusty and a little bent up, that's all. I traded him two screen doors that I got free from a junk man in Honolulu. How's that for a clever fellow?"

Just then did Alice show up, which was just as well, as I might have said something nasty. Alice Finn and her husband Stanley had their small sloop anchored out in the lagoon a short distance from Captain Ernie's old 50-foot yawl.

I hadn't heard the splish-splash of the oars as Alice rowed in—and so there she appeared, balanced on one leg like a stork at water's edge as she bent to slip into sandals before tugging the dinghy up on the beach. Alice—as I knew Stanley to be, for that matter—is a crackerjack seaperson. It had taken a while, to be sure, but both, in this matter of how to make the boating life work, had become clever fellows.

Captain Ernie and I watched Alice tug and grunt as she pulled the dinghy out of the water. We both knew that Alice is not one to court the help of noble males—that, more so, she resents the idea. So we sat and watched, until it became apparent that she was missing a sandal and having to hop along on one foot.

Visually—just to look at it, that is—the lagoon of Majuro is one of the most classic of all the South Pacific. It is the "No Swimming" signs, with their concomitant warnings of pollution, that here puncture illusion's pink balloon—and it was the fear of cutting her foot on the shards of broken beer bottles along the beach that had Alice cursing the loss of a sandal.

"Thanks a lot," she said, when finally Captain Ernie and I got there. But now that we were there and the boat was already out of the water—well, Alice was wanting to have us help her push it back in. She stepped into the boat, took the center seat, took up the oars as if to row, and said, "We've got to get back to the boat before Stanley wrecks the chicken."

"That's what's cooking out there?" said Captain Ernie.

I saw a column of sooty black smoke rising from somewhere in the after section of Alice and Stanley's anchored boat. The boat faced us bow-on, about a hundred yards offshore, and so I couldn't make out exactly where the smoke was coming from. It gave the impression the boat was on fire.

"Hoolie-Hoolie chicken," said Alice. "You'll love it. You baste the chicken in soy sauce, pineapple juice, plenty of minced garlic marinated in rum, and then you cook it over a red-hot hibachi and don't take it off till it just starts to burn. Stanley learned to make it when we were in Hawaii—one of the few things he liked over there. Los Angeles West, he calls it, with the worst freeway planning commission that ever hit the Pacific."

Alice and Stanley (Captain Ernie snorts at all this) have the idea that there are a lot better places to find what boaters like to think of as Paradise, that most of the South Pacific these days appears an extension of some of the less desirable districts of Los Angeles. But that's their view, and ours is not to tell the reader where to go or how to get there in a boat. Even Alice says that's one you've got to figure out for yourself.

As it was that day, I was having to regret my not being able to have lunch with my friends. The fact was, I scarcely had time to help Captain Ernie push the dinghy back in the water. He had his pants bottoms pulled up the way kids have when they're afraid to go home wet, it looked to be. But he got his pants wet anyway after giving a fierce shove and then climbing in behind Alice.

Off they went, Alice pulling expertly at the oars, Captain Ernie looking a bit miffed about this, and then I heard a hoarse whoosh-whoosh, followed by a sort of expiring *whuh*—the sound of Stanley's applying what was no doubt a Coast Guard regulation fire extinguisher to whatever part of the lunch had got out of hand out there. Bon voyage and bon appétit, I bid them with a wave. I had to dash off and catch an Air Force transport jet in which I was to be given a lift back to Honolulu.

They have no correspondent in this far-flung American outpost, and so the *New York Times*, at my request, had assigned me to report a natural disaster that had struck Majuro just hours before. A 25-foot wave, most unusual for these parts, had swept the capital district (no point on this atoll stands more than the height of a man above sea level), knocking out, among other things, radio communication with the rest of the world. I would have to phone in my story from Honolulu, where I was living at the time and, mostly, teaching sailing and navigation while putting together this book.

I left Majuro that day with Captain Ernie still wondering (he would send a postcard to remind me of this) what the hell I was calling this *Captain Nemo's Cookbook* for. Not wanting to leave a man dangling this way—well, I found a recipe in one of the Honolulu papers that featured, of all things, stringbeans—an Italian style concoction requiring a particular brand of premium olive oil, fresh shallots (finely chopped), imported pimientos, a good fresh Romano cheese (grated), with recommendations to serve this with a nice, chilled varietal white wine. Along with the recipe I'd clipped, I sent him a bottle of cheap but good white wine.

Months later, I got back a short note, this from the Fiji Islands, and in it Captain Ernie said,

"The wine was excellent"—for him, an unusual turn of phrase—"but the goddamned salad, when finally I did find all the stuff for it (hell, they told me there wasn't an ounce of Romano cheese to be found one end of Fiji to the other—but I found some anyway), just isn't my cup of tea, if you know what I mean.

"The cook who wrote the recipe may have been a clever fellow, but I sure can tell him a few things about how not to ruin a sailor's day. The guy who wrote that recipe—he was no sea cook.

"So, near as I can figure out, you better not have any of that kind of stuff in the thing you're writing. Give folks the straight scoop. This ain't no hayride you're taking 'em on. They've got to learn to be a bunch of clever fellows.

"Start them out from the beginning, show them what it's all about. No goody-two-shoes how-to book, mind you—give 'em the real McCoy stringbeans, if you get my meaning."

Already has it been suggested that this is a dangerous book—one, that like sex, is bound to get good people in trouble if they're so indiscreet as to take it to heart and act upon it.

Those already caught up in the boating life will, no doubt, want to decide for themselves just how far they want to go with the picture-puzzle tidbits of inside information contained in this book, or whether they want to sell the boat and be done with it once and for all. As for the general public (the aspiring boater—and what else can a person be these days), the words of Captain Nemo, upon showing a visitor about that marvel called the *Nautilus*, probably serve as well as any: "Astonishment will probably become your normal state of mind. It will not be possible for you to be bored at the endless spectacle I shall put before you."

And then he adds, as do we:

"And you shall be my fellow student."

To start from the beginning, though certainly is Captain Ernie Hall wise in suggesting this—that's more easily said than done.

Chapter 2

An Out-of-the-Way Shack That Floats—
And It Had Damned Well Better

Potent Quotes

"Methods! Approaches! Need the junk master steering towards the sea, with the sails of his vessel billowing in the wind, bother his head about alternative modes of propulsion—oars, paddles, punt-poles, tow ropes, engines and all the rest?

Any sort of vessel, unless it founders or pitches you overboard, is good enough to take you to the one and only sea.

Now do you understand?"

Tseng Lao-Weng, sage

"Why live in a phone booth when you can get a ten-room house cheap?"

Captain Ernie Hall, on *his*
way of doing it

INCE TIME BEGAN (and quite likely before that, some of the evidence purports to show) there have been men and women crazed with the notion that if only we can get our hands on a good boat—well, then and only then are we in a position to tell the world to take its folly and go stuff it.

Had Henry David Thoreau been a boating man, his notions of self-sufficiency and independence drawn from the sea, then he might have given us a thoughtful book on the joy and beauty of hauling up sail and making a run for it, along with complete boatbuilding plans and lots of good advice on where to find the materials for it at always-reasonable prices.

Thoreau, alas, was not a boating man, the appointed trappings of his well-meant Walden were clearly rural ones, and such sanctions as it supposes would seem in this day and age about as effective as a No Trespassing sign set in an open field of ripe strawberries.

In fact, where do you go today to put into practice such truly heartfelt advice as Thoreau does hand down—to build a nice out-of-the-way shack in the woods, take out a subscription to *Mother Earth News*, plant a garden, really work at making it all work, and, then, when it looks like it has, grow a fat pumpkin and sit on it to meditate on what truly has had to have been a great achievement?

The problem here is that twenty minutes after you've sat, the Department of Transportation comes honking to get you to move the shack so a goddamned freeway can be run through the garden. The old-timer with the 140 pristine acres surrounding your place has sold out to a condo developer and is moving to Florida.

Toxic wastes, from God knows where, are oozing into the well dug last summer, and acid rain is killing off the lovely Douglas firs set around the shack for the sheer pleasure of their presence. In the field across the way, where in the spring the deer were at least good to look at as they nibbled down the alfalfa, Bolivians are building a jungle warfare training camp.

While you were out back arguing with the county building

inspector, who has already posted a stop-work order on your son's tree house, a spoiled suburban brat with a walrus mustache, a case of Coors, and a Toyota 4 x 4 has run over your pumpkin and squashed it.

But wait, as they say in those marvelous television commercials, this isn't all you get for your investment. The good news is that a Dallas-based franchiser is just dying to put in a combo car wash and video-game operation, a clever tax dodge if ever you've heard one, and what a horrible waste of water and perfectly good electricity. But what the hell, it's an irreversible mess already—and now he's offering cold cash to take Walden off your hands. One is sorely tempted to let the fool have it, take the cash—and go buy a boat.

To be sure, the history of boating tells us, with as much common sense as it has come to possess over the centuries, that to go out and get a boat and get the hell off the land is about the wisest thing a frustrated man can do. Captain Nemo's resounding "Get thee to the bosom of the sea—only there is independence" is, for example, not the talk of a beaten man grumbling over the neighbor's firing up the power lawn mower at 6 a.m. on a Sunday. He means what he says, and the conviction with which he says it is solidly founded on his having given the matter a lot of thought. As boating philosopher, he is neither an idle nor impulsive man.

His submarine *Nautilus*, with its powerful engines that ran practically forever on sodium extracted from the very seas upon which the vessel sank and rose at will, to this day stands as a superb example of what you can do if you've got the money. Indeed, Nemo cruised along with Mozart and Beethoven, at 50 miles an hour sometimes, to the smooth perk and clicking noises of every conceivable technological innovation you can cram into a boat 223 feet long. When submerged, the *Nautilus* displaced 1500.2 metric tons. Nemo, by the way, did not, as some researchers have concluded, make use of the Rühmkorff induction coil, but rather developed one of his own to raise the extreme high voltages he required. No one knows for sure, but it is thought that the Croatian genius Tesla, who developed the technology for the sorry electric chair (Edison, with his inadequate DC system, tried and failed, it appears), borrowed from Nemo in developing *his* high voltages. In Japan, researchers in the new submersible technology dispute this— but what do they know?

In any event, originals by Titian and DaVinci scarcely rattled in their frames during those times when the moody Captain Nemo (most rich geniuses *do* get moody, we have to admit) thundered at an impressive piano-organ installed in the sub's large and well-furnished drawing room, next to which was a library, flooded with light from an invisible source (another "Tesla first" here?), that contained 12,000 volumes of Nemo's favorite books, a racy George Sand novel or two pushed in amongst these.

One thing is obvious, even if we are left to wonder about the rest of it:

Not only has Nemo beaten the system, it appears—he couldn't care less that it even exists. He goes his own way with the grandest of style, with the same tone of absolute confidence as when he tells us his seaweed cigars are every bit as good as "choice Havana."

Nemo makes no mention of the pitfalls of going to a place where boats are sold and making a deal on the first right smart one that catches your eye. Nor does he give us any good tips on how to get the most for your money. He doesn't even mention the Sunday newspaper ads, nor that most boating magazines, usually in the back pages, list all sorts of stuff that is up for sale.

But neither would he have bought property at Walden with a mind to building himself a neat little shack in the woods. He just didn't want to have to deal with this kind of problem.

Chapter 3

Let's Go Shopping

Potent Quotes

*"I think it goes back to one of the great elemental instincts.
Man wants to provide himself with a shelter, and he wants
to build something that will carry him through the ani-
mosity of the natural world, that will guard and preserve
him through vast ocean waves, and nothing else in the
world you can do will come as close to it as building the
perfect boat."*

Bud McIntosh,
New Hampshire boatbuilder

*"This was the first time ever I'd seen someone's transposing
a classic work of science fiction adventure into a backyard
boatbuilding manual. Myself, I kind of liked the idea—and
so did he. But not to put too fine a point on this . . ."*

The Author, one day

I N 1973, SCHOLARS AT a small monastic university near Mt. Ararat created what appears a realistic reconstruction (scaled at roughly an inch to the foot of the original) of Noah's ark. Motivated by the same concerns that must have prompted the craft's builders, they came up with what a modern boat designer has likened to "a very well-built barge indeed that was as much mud sled as it was—sailing craft is not the word for it. There's no indication the original had even a rudder."

Noah, apparently acting on a tip from a high-placed source in the administration of the day, premised the design concept that went into his boat on a theory of total rout: not only was the consumer market rapidly going under—the rapid erosion of available natural resources was making necessary the immediate safe transport of an entire animal kingdom of endangered species. God knows where he was going to end up, and so he ingeniously built accordingly. In this he was not, strictly speaking, a boating man, but rather a determined survivor who set aside a life of farming and animal husbandry to make the best of it in the interim. It was the sea that overtook Noah—not Noah who took to the sea over any great love for it.

All the facts are not yet in, as the history of boating has a distance to go before reaching that time when no more is heard about it. But from the very beginning—the "Dawn," we can say—has the boating man been compelled to ask, without his getting an answer that is scarcely more than a distant echo of the question, "Just what makes a right smart boat, anyway—is not mine better than the next?" Echoes never talk back, they only repeat the question. The principle is well known to mariners who have learned to find their way through fogbound straits, some of these by beating pots and pans together and then counting the number of seconds it takes the racket to get back to them.

Months ago, after a lot of time spent standing around in West Coast backyards and garages and interviewing principals, I got the impression—and it was a happy one—that we'd become a nation of boatbuilders urgently engaged in a grand scheme to escape the cities and suburbs that have become a daily nightmare. The boats varied widely in size, shape, and concept, just as the garages and backyards varied in dictating how large a boat could be built and whether the neighbors would get huffy and start pushing back, usually with calls to the building inspector, sometimes a cop, when the push-and-shove got out of hand. You just don't tell a backyard boatbuilder to lay down his tools and stop banging around all hours of the night.

During the course of this investigation I ran across a hippie who told me that Jules Verne's *Twenty Thousand Leagues Under the Sea* was a whole lot more than the mere kids' book that some critics would have us believe. If you read closely, he said, there is coded into the book everything you need to know to build a mini-*Nautilus*, modeled after the *Nautilus*'s all-purpose work-and-pleasure boat—the crank Nemo's one unfailing delight in life, it does appear.

As the hippie saw it, Nemo was at heart a small-boat man, the *Nautilus* a drag and an awful responsibility, when you got right down to it. In any event, Captain Nemo, in the book, describes his secret dream-boat this way:

> This boat is attached to the upper part of the hull of the *Nautilus*, and occupies a cavity made for it. It is decked, quite watertight, and held together by solid bolts. This latter leads to a manhole made in the side of the boat. By this double opening I get into the small vessel. They shut the one belonging to the *Nautilus*, I shut the other by means of screw pressure. I undo the bolts, and the little boat goes up to the surface of the sea with prodigious rapidity. I then open the panel of the bridge, carefully shut till then; I mast it, hoist my sail, take my oars, and I'm off."

Never again in the book, we have to admit, does Nemo exhort with as much joy and enthusiasm. He reverts to his role as classic romantic exile who would just as soon beat his head against the walls of his submarine as have a nice day.

Captain Ernie Hall, when I told him this story, snorted and said, "His problem was he had too many valves and switches to worry about. The *Nautilus* was a plumber's nightmare. Myself,

I'd have torn all that crap out and thrown it overboard where it belongs." Captain Ernie despises boat plumbing, its intricate miseries, its mysterious breakdowns. His broader philosophical feeling is that boat plumbing and wiring tends to do unto men and women what the Lilliputians did unto Gulliver—"tied him down so that he couldn't move, much less get up and leave. In the boating life, you have to keep it simple and down-to-earth.

"So whatever happened to the hippie?" he wanted to know. "Did he finish the boat or did it finish him?"

Chapter 4

A Matter Of Technique and Intimate Know-How

Potent Quotes

"He who organizes his life can live in Hell and enjoy it."

Advice found in an old
Tibetan boating manual

"Well, there's nothing like a good, old-fashioned sea mystery. It reminds me of the end of the Jules Verne tale, in which Nemo is sucked into a maelstrom off the Norwegian coast—but there's left the little nonsubmersible case with Nemo's studies of the sea. This has never been found, you know. God knows where it drifted to.

Alice Finn, an evening's
bedtime comment

$\mathcal{T}$HE LAGOON BACK THERE at Majuro, with its frustratingly clear but polluted waters—that was not where first I made the acquaintance of Alice and Stanley. I knew them long before they had heard of Hoolie-Hoolie chicken, much less given thought to the possibility that to master the cooking of this somewhat gourmet dish would take more time and patience than sometimes they had. Bean sprouts, grown in plastic bags, and homemade yogurt were far more to their tastes when first we did meet. In those days, they served their stuff right out of the container, no fuss, no mess.

At that time, I was researching a previous book of mine that had to do with cross-country skiing, Zen, sex, and the California lifestyle shortly before and after the Great Arab Oil Embargo that was to leave cars literally stranded along the road. For a time there, it looked as though the whole of civilization, as we know it, had run out of gas.

Alice and Stanley were convinced at the time that this was to be a permanent condition of their Western existence, and so they had taken to living in a homemade teepee up in the California High Sierra, where I ran across them one day while ski touring. Of course I wondered what they were doing up there.

Well, it turned out they'd got hold of a *Whole Earth Catalog*, among other printed how-to source materials of that age, and were embarked on an alternative mode of existence that referred back to Eskimo and Indian cultures, either of which had survived and flourished long before there were cars, tractors, and chain saws, and Arabs monopolizing oil.

From the looks of it, Alice and Stanley were doing a pretty good job of the nuts-and-bolts stuff of surviving in the wilds Indian and Eskimo fashion. But after a while along came another problem to have to cope with. This, it turned out, was a park ranger, who told them they were in a no-camping area within the boundaries of Yosemite National Park. Pronto, he kicked them out and told them to take their teepee with them or he'd damn well burn it. The park was not to be parked in that way. That was the law. "Live like an Indian," said Alice, "and you find out what the Indians learned years ago—sooner or later you're bound to have a run-in with the authorities."

For years I heard not a word of what had become of Alice and Stanley. One rumor had it that Alice was selling Mary Kay cosmetics and was happily with kids in a nice house in the suburbs. Another was that she and Stanley were raising chickens in Petaluma, California, had gone broke (not enough scratch?), and were looking for a cheap boat to buy. The latter turned out to be closer to the truth, which I was happy to discover when one day I ran into her in the back of a large marine hardware store in downtown San Francisco. She was looking for one of those ingeniously simple plastic sextants that sold for about 20 bucks in most stores but was on sale in this one for 12 or 15, as I recall. "Stanley and I are sailing to Hawaii," she told me. "So what's up with you these days?"

On Jules Verne's gravestone, in Amiens, France, is engraved more than mere statistical notice of the death of Captain Nemo's father, to put it one way, in 1905. The additional wordage is Verne's and says, "Onward to Eternal Youth and Immortality." Was at last a Cheshire cat telling us what he knows that we don't? I mention this because Alice had on her face that day a look I can only describe as being of the selfsame stuff. She seemed not to have aged one whit. She was very much the same young woman I had seen sunning naked in front of the teepee that day eons ago, rubbing herself all over with homemade yogurt.

Stanley was in the tent, rubbing himself all over with yogurt too, and I heard him say, "God, this time let's do it in the snow, Alice." Unseen up to now, I discreetly withdrew on skis, quietly making my way through the woods and back to my own camp. So long for now—but not forgotten.

That day I met Alice in the back of the marine hardware, I told her, "This is some coincidence, wouldn't you say? Here you are newly embarked on the boating life, and here I am writing a how-to book about that very thing. Maybe we could exchange pointers. That would be very useful to me, I know."

Well, she agreed to do that, certainly, as she had some views of her own on the subject. But at the moment, she told me, she and Stanley were very busy getting the boat ready. I gave her my current address, which she jotted down on her list of last-minute purchases. When they got settled in Hawaii, she said, she'd write at length and fill me in. "Would you like it double-spaced? Drawings, illustrations?" "No, no," I said. "But if you care to give it a formal theme, how about, *The Art of Converting a Former Recreational Sailboat into a Comfortable, Fulltime Live-aboard with Self-sufficiency and Independence in Mind.* With your background in tenting, you ought to be especially qualified for this. Don't hold back a thing."

"It's a very *small* former recreational sailboat," said Alice. "Not just everybody can learn to love it." We left it at that. Bon voyage. Catch you later.

That's how *this* got started. It would be a mistake, I mean, not to let Alice have her say about these matters. If anything would seem to be missing, it would perhaps be the larger, more objective picture, personalities aside. But then, there isn't room on a postcard to get in more than the few tentative sketches of the just-arrived, and it was a postcard that I got before anything else, a telegraphic tidbit. She said:

> We first thing ran into a guy over here who says he's a pal of yours. Captain Ernie Hall has that huge barge of his anchored down the way from us. He sure likes to talk, but we like him—even if he says it's dumb living on a small boat the way we do. As if having a big boat is the one and only answer to making it in this boating-for-survival business.
>   Did you know that a woman, if she stands up, can pee further than most men can? Stanley was sure surprised, anyway.

Alice's boating philosophy had right-off taken an odd tack, if not a fatal one. I wasn't sure how to "incorporate" this, other than in a tentative way. Suggest to the reader that it has been the history of boating generally that the odd tack is preferred to most other kinds? Surely when an incessant quest for self-sufficiency and independence combines its philosophy with this—that's when you have to sort out the wind from the dust that gets in your sails, no?

Months were to pass before I got an expanded statement from Alice, a whopper. Her letter was the beginning of a motley, muddled correspondence that tempted my giving it an appropriately snide title, as I might a bound but nameless volume that *knew* no bounds, none. Was it she herself who eventually got to calling it *Captain Nemo's Hula-Hula Holiday?* Maybe she did. I don't quite remember. Her letter began simply enough:

Dear Hal,
    I had to stand in line at the Kaneohe post office an hour to buy stamps to get this mailed. It's very crowded over here on the main island of Oahu. The freeways are nuts and you can't find parking anywhere without having to either pay through the nose or through the mail, whichever comes first, the lot attendant with his hand out or the maid with the tickets—not that we own a car or ever again will. A bicycle would seem to be the answer here. The weather's balmy most of the time, the distances between places you need to get to and back short, just as the island itself is short on—'brains,' is not the word. I don't think there is a word for it when people clutter a naturally beautiful island with freeways and cement condos, close windows to shut out the sea breeze so that the air conditioner works at maximum efficiency, then complain that the place has lost its native charm.
    It's difficult to walk 10 feet down the street here without somebody in a cute, sort of McDonald's-Goes-Hawaiian costume coming out from behind a palm and barking, 'Aloha, you've just completed this phase of our King-Kamahamaha-Walked-Here Tour.' That's $3.50, usually. To do this on a bicycle, they charge express rates. If somebody doesn't first steal the bicycle. So no bikes for us here, either. When we can, we walk. This is the Mystery Spot of the Pacific, but only a dry cleaner could divine how it got that way.
    The main reason I write is not to spoil your day with this, but to say I hope to hell this book you're writing isn't going to be just another goddamned how-to book—one of those stone-carved jobs that tries to tell you there's only one way to cook a chicken and what pot to cook it in. Not that I don't like chicken, you understand.
    Still, it's a chicken-shit boating book that doesn't have a strong viewpoint about boating. That goes with the territory. May I suggest one, then give you a little time to think on it?
    Actually, I've got two ideas for you. One is to make what you're able from this, which is a saying of one of the true greats of the old-time Tibetan school of boating: *He who organizes his life can live in hell and enjoy it.* There's a whole lot to go on here, if you know that it was a very happy man who said this.

As for my other idea, I'm not sure I can put it in so succinct a way. There's too much texture to it, for one—like an abstract idea walking around in a fur coat that keeps changing color every time you try to describe it. But you've got to start somewhere. I will.

A couple of days ago, we got stuck on a reef in Kaneohe Bay. We sailed right onto it because somebody had taken the plastic Clorox bottle off the warning marker, and Stanley saw only the bare stick sticking up, which didn't mean anything to him until it was too late to bear off.

Kaneohe Bay, it should be pointed out, is on the windward side of the island of Oahu in the northern section of the Hawaiian chain. The bay, though warm and shallow and with channel depths of up to 27 feet, is strewn with coral reefs, only a few of which are marked, and many of these by sticks and poles topped with inverted Clorox bottles. Usually damned small ones. The reef Alice refers to is a large one just off Coconut Island at the south end of the bay, at a point where the channel abruptly narrows.*

Alice goes on to say that their 28-foot fiberglass cutter (originally a factory-rigged sloop, it was changed over as a matter of personal preference), with a fin keel that draws just over four feet, ran onto the reef and was stuck there—but only for a time, it is her point.

The noise the keel made when it ground across the coral was sickening—like the bottom of the boat was coming off. But the thing is, we dropped the sails pronto, put on our Adidas, got out of the boat, waded to the bow and pushed. It took only about ten minutes of push and shove to get back in the channel and on our way again. The only thing damaged was Stanley. Some people were looking on and he figured he had made a fool of himself for running onto the reef in the first place.

Having chalked a point for her side, Alice now taunts the opposition, which is Captain Ernie Hall. She has this to say:

When Ernie ran that 15-ton scow of his on the reef, the Clorox bottle was on the marker stick then, but he had been having a few drinks that night. He was stuck there four days.

---

*The author has often scraped this particular reef.

In fairness to Captain Hall, it must be said that Alice's description of his boat is not altogether accurate. Called *Roundabout*, Captain Hall's 50-foot yawl does weigh slightly over 15 tons, is wood-planked in the old style that requires frequent caulking, and though of nondescript design, does bear some resemblance to Joshua Slocum's famed *Spray* (another whole school of boating thought here) when seen from a distance when under full sail and smartly but slowly (resolutely is the word) plugging along in a good, stiff wind from off the beam. As to what happened next, after Captain Hall ran *Roundabout* on the reef, Alice does give a fair-minded accounting:

> He was too proud to hire a tug and his boat was too big to push. So he just sat out there for four days, reading his Mark Twain and drinking beer while he waited for the right combination of wind and tide to come along—and then he sails off the reef with a look on his face to make you think he planned the whole thing.
>
> I have to admire the way he gets around in that thing—but when it comes to lifting and pushing and getting a move-on quick, he's got a semi-truck with twelve flat tires. That's what, not Li Po, but that other advocate of the keep-it-small, keep-it-light school meant when he said, 'Don't trust anything you can't lift with your own two hands.' Stanley says Al Capone said that, but he's just trying to be funny.

Actually, it was Thoreau who made the remark to which Alice refers, and though he didn't have strict application to the boating life in mind, he might well have been thinking of a canoe to paddle about in on Walden Pond. The principle of the thing holds true in any instance, and it is Alice certainly who uses it to tell us why she thinks their 28-footer (they had bought this used and had spent quite some time fixing it up to meet certain standards of theirs) is the ideal getaway boat. She goes on about this, after explaining at last, that Captain Ernie's much earlier remark, "It's dumb," refers to his near-fanatical preference for a large boat of traditional design.

> For him—six-foot four and the way he lurches and bangs around when he's got a few drinks under his belt—thinking small is out of the question. 'Why live in a phone booth,' he cackles, 'when you can get a ten-room house cheap?'

Well, for one thing, the last lady friend he had on that 50-foot barge of his couldn't stand the mess and left. It's all the junk he collects. His latest acquisition is a bunch of trashed-out screen doors that he thinks he can take to the Marshall Islands and sell to a Japanese house remodeler he knows down there. God, he's got over a hundred of them stashed down below—and then he comes over to our boat and raves about how great it is to have a big boat with plenty of elbow room. Stanley says the only reason he comes over here is so he can find a place to sit without having to shove screen doors out of the way.

I don't mean to say that Captain Ernie doesn't have his act together, because he has in lots of ways that are downright amazing sometimes.

Captain Hall's handling of the situation on the reef, we ought to mention, certainly puts him in good stead in that nautical hall of fame associated with right-smart tradition. The trick he used was established by seamen centuries ago, though generally the custom is to make the extra effort of planting an anchor some distance from the boat and then attempting to "kedge off" by hauling in on the anchor line.

Obviously Captain Hall had no dates or deadlines weighing his mind and was content to wait it out. What is interesting to note at this point is that Jules Verne had Captain Nemo take precisely the same tack when the *Nautilus* ran aground in the dangerous Torres Strait that separates New Guinea and Australia. That situation was critical.

Professor Arronnax, the *Nautilus*'s captive guest and something of a fussbudget, greatly feared the loss of the vessel. But Captain Nemo, "cool and calm," announced his intentions to wait it out. There would be no anchors and no winches put to use—only the Captain's exacting calculations of sun and tide. The *Nautilus* is not lost, Nemo tells his worried guest. "It will carry you yet into the midst of the marvels of the ocean."

Once again, we see, does boating philosopher Nemo inspire utter confidence. He knows the game inside and out, and he, above all, is the master player. Neither wind nor tide, and certainly no shark boat salesman, will ever get the best of him. Others of us are known to take what we can get—and then later marvel that it didn't work out quite as expected. Right smart is right on, depending on where you get your advice. . . .

PART II

PUNTING TO BYZANTIUM:
A GEM FOR ALL SEASONS

Chapter

Wind Shapes

Potent Quote

"Raib appears in the doorway of the deckhouse and gazes balefully to windward. The sea, roiled suddenly by squall, turns a soft black. Soon rain is pelting on the deckhouse roof, running off in wind-shaped strings. Raib cups it in his hand and splashes his face, then drinks some, gasping.

I tell you, Vemon, to drink fresh rain dat way is something good."

Peter Matthiessen,
Far Tortuga

AUTHOR-ACTOR-SAILOR STERLING Hayden's book *The Wanderer* remains a classic sea tale still, and in it he tells the story of his schooner voyage to Tahiti, to whisk his children out-of-country in defiance of a court order remanding the children's custody elsewhere. Captained by one Spike Africa, a rare old salt whose feats of sail had got him named President of the Pacific, Hayden's *Wanderer*, sails high and reef lines slipped, slipped unnoticed through the San Francisco Bay fog early one morning and got away.

Obviously Hayden is a great admirer of getaway boats of old-time, classic intent. Indeed is such a boat, its slipping out of the clutches as it did, potently symbolic of the need to be captain of one's own destiny, whatever the kind of adversity we would seek to escape by sailing away in one.

Hayden and I were sitting one day in the railroad car he was living in at the time. It had formerly belonged to a railroad president and was fixed up to be home and office. Now it sat parked on a siding in downtown Sausalito. We were talking about boats when suddenly he blurted out that anyone who pays more than $2,000 for one is a sucker.

He was not talking about sailing dinghies, mind you, but honest-to-God big boats. Venerable old-time schooners, North Sea pilot boats, Netherlander canal barges with folding masts and leeboards. The classic real McCoy, in other words, such as befits the traditional notion of both the romance and the practicalities of the deep sea boating life.

The trick, said Hayden, is to go to Nova Scotia, say—or to most any other out-of-the-way maritime province, such as the Florida Keys or the northern coast of Maine. One seeks out bayous and backwaters, the nooks and crannies along almost any back-country coastline, U.S.A. These days, inflation always on our heels, it does take a bit of looking. And when you do find one, it's going to be a fix'er-upper.

At a wonderfully tucked-away little harbor called Aldo's, somewhere along "the coast," we find one (an old, wood classic, that is), and it is called the *Marie Celeste*. Early this morning, just as the sun was dispersing the last of a classically post-dawn sea mist, Aldo himself rowed us out to the moorage to have us step aboard and have a close look at it. Aldo owns the marina here, runs a sales brokerage on the side.

The boat's a downright steal, Aldo confides while picking at his teeth with the corner of one of his business cards. The owner, a young man in his twenties, will take a good, used VW camper-van in trade, and Aldo will call it fair and square if the buyer will agree to pay the small commission Aldo requires to swing the deal and do the paperwork and such. The only reason the kid is selling the boat, says Aldo is—well, it's the girlfriend. They used to live on it till she made 'em move off because she's got no place to do this tie-dye stuff she's into. The kid—he's sick about it. "But you know how that goes. It was either her or the boat."

Sure, Aldo, we know how that goes.

Down below, on the *Marie Celeste* riding at anchor in the mist, we had entered into another world when this morning Aldo rowed us out to have a look at her. There was the rich patina of old wood and weathered varnish, the faint smell of old seawater that has distilled in the bilge to a musky liqueur. Gaff-rigged, Tahiti ketch, Colin Archer North Sea pilot boat, turn-of-the-century Chesapeake oysterman—it is all of these things, composited into one hell of a venerable wood classic.

Considered from another angle—well, they built things good in 1937, says Aldo encouragingly. The *Marie Celeste*, he tells us, was built of solid oak frames and hand-sawn fir planks, along the British Columbia coast, by two eccentric but gifted brothers who "really knew their stuff."

Now, 42 years later, the only reason the *Marie Celeste* is listing to starboard at the moment—and Aldo assesses the angle to be "maybe only four degrees," though other observers have put the figure at ten—is that the caretaker, Aldo's teenage son, left the main hatch open the last time it rained. Matter of fact, Aldo is sending the kid out to pump the boat this very afternoon, he says. We wish he'd done this before we got here. As Aldo shows us through the main saloon, the floorboards on the starboard side are making squishy noises.

Blackish water is oozing up between the floorboard seams. This is greasy and slick, but we know to get through it okay by avoiding stepping on the stuff.

Besides, this is a small thing indeed if we consider that the *Marie Celeste* is certainly priced right. What's more, it's a fix'er-upper, and this, we know, holds promise of its being a potent object of great personal commitment over a wonderfully long time of love and tinkering. Then, when we will have got the thing finished, will come that marvelous sense of completion and fulfillment that eludes most of modern man as the result of his and her having usually 9-to-5 jobs that go on forever and yet accomplish nothing of lasting satisfaction. This considered, we are psychologically on pretty solid ground here.

For the sake of classic authenticity, from the situation as it clearly stands now and on down through the chain of events that we can predict to follow as night follows day, we make a modest switch of personages here. We are replacing ourselves with a couple named Sid and Alexis, while cautiously we back into the wings and watch from a distance. Sid and Alexis's case is an actual one, as is that of the *Marie Celeste*'s curious impact on their lives, though names and circumstances have been changed somewhat. That their situation, as it evolves, is as typical as it is universal we can say without having to change a thing.

Sid and Alexis are not veteran boating people. But they do have a knowledgeable friend who owns a refurbished classic boat and has several times on weekends over the years taken Sid and Alexis sailing.

Sid runs a small but going motorcycle customizing and repair shop. Alexis teaches crafts part time at a Montessori day school not far from their house in the suburbs. Both are in their late thirties and for years now have been looking for a *Marie Celeste*: something cheap but classic that they can fix up themselves over an extended time, with sailing off to Bora Bora firmly in mind when the work is done.

Already, at an annual nautical flea market (bargains in used marine gear galore) has Sid bought for a dollar a British Admiralty chart of the Bora Bora coastline. Not only is the chart up to date, like British charts generally it has an antique quality about it that comes of all the contour markings, the carefully sketched symbols depicting both shoals and prominent landmarks useful to piloting one's way safely into an exotically foreign port.

Aldo, our unassuming and friendly broker, owns the nearby Lighthouse Cafe, which is an essential feature of Aldo's delightfully tucked-away marina, where Sid and Alexis have just finished the "Fisherman's Special," as it is called on the menu. Two eggs anyway you like 'em, plump sausage patties, plenty of hash browns, all the coffee refills you can drink for the price of the first cup. After such a breakfast, even the grease goes down well. One feels right with the world. "And damn it," Sid tells Alexis, both looking through the cafe window, "it does look good out there, even if it does list." The *Marie Celeste* rides indifferently at anchor, while Aldo, sitting in the booth's other side, brushes crumbs of buttered toast from off the sales contract he has drawn up for their inspection.

Aldo has agreed to accept $500 earnest money, on the condition insisted on by Sid and Alexis that the purchase of the boat be contingent upon a safisfactory marine survey. This advice they got from the veteran boating friend. For an investment of $75, in this instance, plus the surveyor's mileage to and from the not-too-distant metropolitan area (a "good man" recommended by the boating friend, and thus worth the additional $35.70 in travel costs, it is hoped), Sid and Alexis have tentatively insured themselves against buying a worthless hulk. If the surveyor's news is bad news, then they have the choice of asking the owner to bring the boat up to snuff or of turning down the deal altogether and getting back the $500. This procedure is wisely a standard one.

Several weeks have passed. Our surveyor, as are most, is a very busy fellow. But at least has Aldo kept up his end of the deal and cranked the *Marie Celeste* out of the water on his wonderfully funk marine railway that uses the same donkey engine that once ran Aldo's father's sawmill. Eventually the surveyor shows up and the *Marie Celeste* is gone over from stem to stern, truck to keelson, fitting by fitting.

The surveyor has reported dry rot in the transom* (the whole thing has to be replaced, as a matter of fact), sprung planks in several key places, with new fastening for the entire hull recommended. The keel bolts, unfortunately, are all but rusted through and causing bad leaks, the auxiliary engine is frozen up with rust (a complete overhaul recommended here), some sails rotted, some necessary ones missing from the owner's inventory, more dry rot under the length of the toerail (stem to stern, replace both sheer strakes while you're at it, it is recommended), most of the bronze through-hull fittings are "gone."

There is a remarkably long list of "little things" that need either fixing or replacement: turnbuckles, blocks, shroud fittings, most of the shrouds, in fact, and so on. From one standpoint, the surveyor tells Sid and Alexis, "You've got a deficit on your hands," to the tune of $41,000 if indeed they plan to bring the boat up to snuff and standards of safe sea passage. From another standpoint, he encourages them: they're getting a hell of a lot of boat for the money. In the main, Sid and Alexis are now at a critical watershed.

What they must do now is to decide whether to go ahead with the deal regardless, wondering as they do: does the bargain price offset the cost of the fixing, in the end is it worth it, do we have the time, where do we get $41,000? Affecting the latter consideration is, importantly, another: should they hire out the repairs with the knowledge, which they have, that boat repairmen, like car mechanics, don't accept time payments? Even if the hired work is done incrementally, over an extended time, still it will be cash on the barrel head each time around— with inflation holding its hand out too, as the weeks, months, possibly years, of yard time and labor tick past on the way to getting the whole job done.

It is broker Aldo who encourages their taking the obvious alternative—the plan that Sid and Alexis had pretty much decided on before they found the ailing *Marie Celeste*, and

---

*Dry rot is a wood disease, a kind of freshwater induced leprosy, that does not infect fiberglass. Fiberglass boats have their own problems.

which was an essential feature of their get-an-old-classic-and-get-away scheme at the very outset of formulating it. Only they hadn't budgeted $41,000 in fix-it funds. "Like I been saying," intones Aldo, "hell, do it yourself on weekends. I've got everything you need here."

For an out-of-town marine supplies franchiser (Aldo is also franchiser of two Coke machines, a candy dispenser and a "fresh frozen bait concession"), Aldo's inventory is really not all that bad and includes all the canned and standard quickie fix-it items, certainly. He's got the recommended Gluvit stuff (the epoxy sealer that "finds and stops leaks" that might otherwise require hours of tedious and expensive repairs), ABC Metal Cleaner, Mold Away spot remover in a handy spray can, Paint-A-Carpet—the works. Like most quickie fix-it nautical items dispensed in cans and bottles, ounce per ounce is the price nearly that of gold. Gluvit, for instance, is about $10 the quart. But within certain limitations it does at least work.

At the moment, Aldo is recommending a quick going-over with the Gluvit stuff while the boat is still out of the water and up on his ways now, shortly after the surveyor's inspection. "Hell," chortles Aldo, with the acumen of the backwater franchiser who knows his products, "all you do is swat the stuff on like painting the side of a barn. *It* finds the leaks. All *you* do is be sure you get enough on there."

"If we can fix the leaks," Sid tells Alexis at this time of critical decision, "at least we can live aboard without getting our feet wet. That will save our having to rent an apartment or something while we fix up the rest of it.

"If we sell the equity in the house, that will give us eighteen thousand in do-it-yourself fix-it money. The commute to work won't be all that bad. About an hour each way, I figure."

So far, the plan makes good sense. Alexis agrees with this. But she is left to wonder whether the condition the boat is in just now rules against their living aboard it. The former owner, for instance, left behind an unfinished shower stall, a plumber's nightmare of pipes, tubes, and a rust-plugged shower head, with no drain and no sign of an exterior water hook-up. The galley, such as it is, consists of a charming, cast-iron cookstove with the firebox burned out, a curious sink made of three pine boards with a large, round hole in the center that empties into a bucket set below. "And what do we do about the laundry?" asks Alexis.

"Hell, we got all that here," says Aldo. "For a lifetime membership, which will cost you only two big ones, you got the clubhouse to use. Aldo's Yacht Club, they call it. Shower, propane cookstove. No cake oven, though. But wouldn't be at all surprised if my wife, if you asked, will let you use hers. As for a laundromat, we got two machines out back of the clubhouse. Wife runs that concession. They take quarters."

"Sounds better all the time," says Sid.

As marinas go, Aldo's has a definite backwater charm about it. Sid and Alexis are thinking pretty much the same thing just now. There are trees and picnic tables, very little traffic along the winding road that skirts the broad point on which Aldo's park, as it were, stands by the tidewater slough called Farley's. Not a bad place to live, really—or to camp out, rather, during the interim of fixing up the boat. The region is notorious for sudden heavy rains, dripping fogs that stop cars dead, but then is there a certain charm in that, to be sure, a rich sense of aquatic isolation from the troubles of the world. When the sun does come out here, it is downright glorious. Like today, for instance. Sid and Alexis buy the boat and, on the spot, five quarts of Gluvit. Aldo is beginning to like these nice folks. "Ten percent off on the Gluvit," he says. The deal is signed and sealed. Sid and Alexis are, to be sure, now the owners of the old wood classic, the *Marie Celeste.*

Chapter

Suddenly by Squall

Potent Quote

*"I tell you, Vemon, to drink fresh rain dat way is some-
thing good."*

Peter Matthiessen
Far Tortuga

$\mathcal{T}$HIS IS GOING TO be more fun than I thought," says Alexis late one evening as she is taking her first hot shower in the back rooms of Aldo's Yacht Club headquarters, the main building of which used to be Aldo's father's Richfield service station.

The shower, of which there is but one, his and hers, has been rigged up, is the word for it, in the tiny former storage room off the side of Gramp Aldo's repair garage. Sid and Alexis are in the shower together and lathering one another after a hard day's work on the boat, and this is what much of the fun is about.

The *Marie Celeste* is house and home now, a mutual *cause célèbre* that is, at least for Sid, a hell of a lot more exciting than his having to mow the lawn Sundays back in bland suburbia.

It was their very decision to live aboard, to save money on rent, to be close to their work, to enjoy a newfound life on the water, they have come to conclude, that dictated what on the boat should be fixed first. In this case it was the decks, with the decision made when came the unexpected drencher in July— the one month, Aldo had told them, you could depend on having good sun and clear skies, perfect weather for getting the decks fixed. Came the rain (Rangoon? Calcutta?), that was the night Sid had to rig up sheets of plastic, in the manner of tents, over their bunks in the forepeak. God knows how many quarts of Gluvit had already been applied—and still the decks leaked. But the tents over their bunks did at least keep the bedding dry.

Now, Sid has decided to replace the deck altogether, on the advice of the veteran sailing friend, who came to visit one day and scoffed that what Sid had on his hands was hopeless. "That's what I had to do with my boat—tear it all out and start from scratch," he said. Well, the Gluvit hadn't worked, thought Sid, and there were a few or more gaps between the deck planks that looked to be more structural problems than mere caulking ones.

So Sid did the right thing and began poking around a bit, beginning his quest in the stern sheets, where the problem looked to be worse than it was elsewhere. He went so far as to pull up a plank or two, only to discover that underneath were the timbers badly riddled with dry rot. These he would have to replace altogether, and then up in the bows he pulled more planks. "Good God," he came to shout. Not only would the old deck have to come off, the whole damned system of supporting timbers would have to be replaced. To do this—and to do it right—that was going to be a fulltime job, Sid came to realize, when one night he was browsing the Sears, Roebuck catalog looking for the power tools he would need to get the job done before the fall rains hit with vengeance. This brought him face to face with another problem: the dock to which the *Marie Celeste* was now tied and for which they monthly paid $125 did not have the power hook-up to run the table and jig saw, the sander, and the drill Sid figured he would need.

The only available power hook-up was in the shed next to Aldo's marine railway. The shed's roof didn't leak, there was ample room to set up shop inside. Aldo could haul the boat out and set it right next to the shed, thought Sid. What could be more convenient!

"You could do that," said Aldo, when approached with the idea. "'Cept the donkey engine don't work no more." Hauling the huge *Marie Celeste* out of the water for the marine inspection of several months ago had "sprung the goddamned main bearing," Aldo explained.

Well, okay, he could get across that bridge, figured Sid, by setting up shop aboard the *Marie Celeste* and throwing a tarp over the deck to keep the rain out. So he bought a used Honda gasoline power generator for $1,200, the table and jig saw, the sander, the drill. "Sawdust makes me sneeze," said Alexis. "Get a shop vacuum too." Sid got the shop vacuum. Also, the kerosene lamps they were using nights to light the boat's interior were giving Alexis headaches. Sid bought extension cords and several electric wall lamps that did in fact provide a pleasant kind of mood lighting when at last was he set up in the main saloon and running the saw nights.

But the very act of standing there at the electric table saw and cutting the forms he desperately needed to fix the deck was bringing on another problem. The boat was leaking below the waterline and this was making his feet wet. Most of the water was coming in through the stuffing box in the engine compartment. Leaks came from around the keel bolts, too, but these were minor, as were the other ones, though he had no idea where, all in all, the other minor ones were coming from. To determine this, he would have to have the boat hauled out of the water.

Things had been okay before he got the electric saw, as he had had to pump out the bilge but once or twice a week to prevent the water's rising above the floorboards. Now, if daily he didn't remember to pump out the bilge—well, "You're going to get yourself electrocuted," said Alexis.

Indeed, Sid's hand tingled (zipped but not zapped?) when one night he stepped on a squishy floorboard just as he bent to switch on the saw's motor. That did it. "The first thing we're going to do around here is fix that goddamned stuffing box," Sid told Alexis.

The next thing, Sid recalls, was that Alexis got to looking over the checking and savings account books during a dinner of Campbell's Cream of Mushroom soup cooked over a can of Sterno (more early rains this year,—Sid had not quite got around to fixing up the galley cookstove, and the walk through the mud to the Lighthouse Cafe was not worth the Chiliburger Supreme being featured that evening). Alexis remarked that the sale of the equity of the house in the suburbs had netted them only $16,000 (an overlooked mortgage against Sid's motorcycle shop had prevented their realizing more). But the point was, Alexis noted, that of the $16,000—damn it, only $7,000 remained. She mentioned this to Sid, just as he was sipping dregs of mushroom soup, quite cool now, from a coffee mug.

It was not that Alexis had not kept a measured accounting of the money being spent. It was that she *had* kept a careful accounting indeed, item by item, receipt after receipt—and still this didn't explain why and where all the money had gone in so short a time. "And so goddamned little to show for it," shouted Sid.

And they hadn't even gone sailing yet, for the simple reason they had not got around to replacing the missing mainsail, since they had decided to wait until they had funds to replace all the sails (those they did have on hand didn't look as though they would hang in there in any kind of breeze at all), which was going to be quite a costly undertaking. Most of the rigging, and the rot in the foot of the foremast, needed to be fixed if they were going to go sailing with any confidence that the whole business might not come toppling down and wreck the new sails, were they to spend the four thousand necessary to *get* new sails.

"You just have to hang in there," Alexis and Sid's veteran sailing friend advised one bright Sunday when he came up from the city to have a look at the progress they were making.

"It was the same thing with my boat," he encouraged. His, too, was an old wood classic, in this instance a wholly refurbished one that looked like new and sailed marvelously, as refurbished old classics indeed do.

But then he, a young and upcoming partner in a prominent corporate law firm, had gobs of money. Not only had he hired expert craftsmen, he had called in a prominent naval architect whom he charged with seeing that the work was historically authentic. "But that's not necessary in this case," he assured Sid. "Your boat—I dunno. Myself, I kinda like it. Main thing is you better get that stuffing box fixed."

"Goddamn it, I will," said Sid. He was tired of having wet shoes all the time, and Alexis was complaining of stuffed nasal passages caused by the constant damp. The electric heater she had bought and which blew out generator fuses when she turned it on high—that wasn't helping much, either. "We need a good dry fire in here," she reminded Sid. "I thought by now you'd have the wood stove fixed."

The next day, matter of fact, when he was in the city and at the motorcycle shop (actually was he most of that day welding parts to make the new firebox for the galley stove), he called a marine mechanic highly recommended to him by the veteran sailing friend.

Small item, this stuffing box, that is supposed to seal out the sea where the engine driveshaft passes through the hull on the way to linking up with the screw. To the kneebone is connected the thighbone, to the thighbone is connected the

... Well, as the marine mechanic explained it, "probably the shaft's bent, which means chronic trouble with the whole thing."

An admirably thorough craftsman of the old school, the mechanic told Sid it was no use talking about it over the phone. "I'd better come up myself and have a look."

Well, what the hell, thought Sid. The mechanic's day fee wasn't so much that it wouldn't be worth the gain if the old boy could tell him how to fix the stuffing box. Alexis might carp awhile—but not after he got the leak fixed.

The mechanic came up and took the promised thorough look. "Just like I figured," he said. "Bent driveshaft."

"Problem is, though, just fixing the stuffing box won't solve the problem." The bent shaft, it turned out after thorough examination, had been caused by loose engine mountings caused by dry rot in the mountings themselves. Not an uncommon problem in old, wood classics, Sid was told.

"While you're at it," the mechanic advised, "—hell, that old 1939 Studebaker engine you got in there is all froze up (rigor mortis?). Long as you're going to have to haul the boat out, better get that fixed up too."

"Haul out the boat?" said Alexis.

"Lot cheaper to have you come down to my place than to have me come up here," said the mechanic.

Well, that much was to their favor. Even Alexis, despite the cost figures that rolled through her mind like digits in the little window of a service station gas pump, was growing rather fond of the idea of having the boat out of the water. And once it was out of the water, chorused Sid, what would be a better time to fix *all* the leaks below the waterline? That fixed, then would Sid be able to run the saw nights without risk of electrocuting himself. Alexis's sinuses would clear, and now that Sid had all but finished the firebox . . . .

There was, however, another small problem. There always is, of course. This particular one went like this: The kind of professional tug service that Sid and Alexis really ought to hire would cost about $250 a day, which was as long as it was going to take to haul the leaking *Marie Celeste* twelve miles down Farley's Slough and then down the always choppy and windy bay and onto the mechanic's haul-out facilities along the city waterfront. Not being amongst the best of well-preserved quaint elderlies, the *Marie Celeste* would need tender and loving care at the hands of an expert tug crew.

It was Aldo who came up with an alternative plan that would save Sid and Alexis lots of money. He knew of a "goddamned doozy of an outfit," as later Sid would characterize the bunch, that would tow them down to the mechanic's place and back again for less than a professional tug would charge for one way only.

Aldo arranged it all. He made the several phone calls necessary to his reaching the tug's captain at a girlfriend's house. A commitment was given to do the whole job, down the slough and return, for $150 cash provided the money was put up front. "You furnish the insurance," said the captain.

"They're nice fellas," Aldo told Sid. "They'll be here Monday, eight o'clock sharp."

"Good," said Sid. "That gives us the weekend to relax." And what a marvelous end-of-September weekend it was.

Alexis, in fact, saw the break they were getting on the tug fee as a happy omen. There was that onrush of fresh air that comes when you've made a decision to get a nagging problem out of the way even if it is going to cost you money—as in ordering a new muffler installed on the car, having the drain pipes routed out, getting the show on the road, the tent patched, the leak in the garden hose fixed.

That Sunday night, on the eve of the tug's arrival at Aldo's, the sky was clear and there was a full moon casting a romantic light all through the interior of the *Marie Celeste*. Though much of the moon's awesome light came in through the gaping holes in the deck, the night was glorious. A classically diaphanous sea mist cloaked the harbor and gave its own glad light to that of the moon's as down below Sid and Alexis snuggled in the forward V-berth, over a quilt fashioned of two zipped-together flannel and polyester sleeping bags fluffed and fresh from a trip to Aldo's Yacht Club dryer that afternoon. A rare moment of embracing respite was well in hand. Two months after the night, Alexis would visit the doctor and be pronounced pregnant.

As promised, the tug *Panama Banana* arrived at 8 o'clock the next morning. Sid noticed first thing that it was painted in the peculiar colors of silver-aluminum (like sprucing up a rusted old stove pipe?) and canary yellow (the bird sitting on the pipe?), the yellow part being a strange, two-story, boxlike deckhouse built onto the recognizable deck of what appeared to be an old time harbor tug retired out of service in probably the early '40s. Nice.

The *Panama Banana*'s huge screw churned forth a wake like breaking river rapids as the tug swung a sharp one-eighty and presented its stern sheets to Sid, who stood at the bow of the *Marie Celeste* waiting to receive the thick manila towline; the running end and several wraps of which two crewmen had already heaved his way. The line fell short, hit the water with a splash.

A very large face with a thick red beard and frizzed mop of red hair thrust itself from out of the second story window at the back of the tug's deckhouse. It looked to Sid like an old house window, salvaged from a wrecking yard probably, and the man standing in it had had to wrestle with the pull-shade and then tug and grunt to get the lower pane up.

"Captain Wally here," he said. "Today Monday?"

"Last I heard," said Sid. "Why?"

"Hey, dip-shit," Captain Wally shouted at one of the crewmen. "Get that line out of the water." He pulled the window shut with a bang and then vanished behind the brown plastic curtain.

The two crewmen in the tug's stern sheets hauled in the towline, made several wraps of it, and then heaved it. The line fell short of Sid's grasp, hit the water, had to be hauled in again, heaved again, and then, finally, tied to the end of a long pole and passed to Sid as the tug drew close and two crewmen ducked and bobbed to avoid the *Marie Celeste*'s very long bowsprit.

Sid tied the line firmly to the *Marie Celeste*'s partially rotted samson post, whose oak stub rose from the foredeck like a clothesline pole broken off just above the ground. On second thought, Sid called for more line. Though samson posts are ruggedly designed with tow jobs in mind, this particular one wasn't going to take the strain, Sid feared. He intended putting several wraps about the post and then, for extra measure, several more about the foremast.

But the *Panama Banana*, without forewarning, began to pull away, slowly at first, its huge screw churning up mud from the bottom, so that little by little the towline drew taut. Suddenly it was apparent to Sid that the tow job was underway in earnest. The two crewmen had vanished from the tug's stern sheets, leaving no one to hear him, apparently, as Sid shouted, "Hold it, goddamn it. Hold it. I need more line."

Alexis, startled by the way the boat had lurched and made her spill her cup of coffee down the front of her sweatshirt, came from below decks to cup her hand to her mouth too and join Sid in shouting at the tug. "What's the big hurry?" she shouted. "Slow down. Slow down."

"Stop, for chrissake! Stop!" shouted Sid.

The samson post began to creak and groan as, picking up good speed now, the *Panama Banana* rounded the point separating Aldo's tranquil harbor waters from the main channel of Farley's Slough. Quickly was the channel marker left behind in the growing boil of wake of the *Panama Banana* and the *Marie Celeste* combined.

"My God, are they deaf, dumb, and blind?" said Alexis.

The roar of the *Panama Banana*'s big diesel, the blaring away of *Country Joe & The Fish* from the stolen car stereo mounted on the pilothouse wall all but deafened all who were gathered there as Captain Wally passed around a Thai stick and cold bottles from a washtub full of cracked ice and Dos Equis beer bought specially for the occasion.

Wally's girlfriend Samantha, six-foot one, honey-colored braids hanging almost to the hem of a leather miniskirt hiked up to expose plump cheeks encased in a body stocking of white fishnet, toked on a plain old joint stuck in her mouth like a cowboy's hand-rolled Bull Durham. High-heeled pigskin "fashion" boots strained to contain overweight calves as she manned the tug's big wooden wheel while Wally and the boys, Neat Pete and Geronimo Jack, his crew of two, whooped it up.

What they were whooping it up about had Samantha

concerned. Ever since Wally had got the idea, she had been dead set against going into the tug boat business. The last job had been a disaster, and already had Wally got notice to appear in court to explain, if he could, why the Panama Banana Towing and Wrecking Company was not entitled to have its ass sued off.

There was a lot at stake here, a lot was in hock. There was the tatoo parlour in Oakland, the used car parts gig Wally was running out of the old school bus. And now the bank was on their ass about the tug payments.

The needle of the *Panama Banana*'s official knot meter stood on the six mark and Samantha damned well meant to keep it there. Wally was too impatient, too quick to flit from one thing to the next. And now, coming into view from around the bend and about three hundred yards ahead, was the Walnut Grove drawbridge, she thought it was, which she could see was just beginning to lower after having admitted through a large seagoing tug with a string of trailing barges.

She knew the *Panama Banana*'s deckhouse not to be so tall in the sky that it couldn't squeak through even if the bridge were closed all the way. But the sailboat *Marie Celeste* dragging along behind, with its tallest mast a good ten feet higher than the tip of the stereo antenna sticking up from the top of the tug's pilothouse—that, she worried, might be a problem.

"Hey, Wally," she shouted over the goddamned racket in the pilothouse, "—what do I do now? Give 'em four blasts on the horn? How do you make 'em keep it open?"

Wally peered over Samantha's shoulder and out through the pilothouse window. He saw the bridge's main span lowering down, and he took quick action. He grabbed the engine throttle and rammed it forward all the way.

There was a bad bearing and the engine began to pound like a high speed mill press stamping out truck fenders. Even with all the noise, Samantha could hear the pilothouse decking rumble and hum the way walls do at the start of a bad earthquake, and it was making the heels of her boots click and rattle.

Wally was elated by all this. "Ten knots, going on twelve," he shouted. "Look at this thing go! Whoeeee! Mama's waiting at the airport and here comes Papa like he got wings on his shoes and knows how to fly."

Despite herself, Samantha was impressed. She had never seen the tug go like this before. But she wasn't so bowled over that she wasn't still thinking.

"Wally," she shouted. "You know, Wally, if we don't make that bridge on time, we're going to shorten somebody's masts and they aren't going to like that. No way are they going to like that."

"Here, gimme the wheel," shouted Wally. "You blow the ass off the horn. We're going through like gangbusters."

Sid, to be sure, had spotted the lowering drawbridge ahead. He had looked up at the masts, back at the bridge, up at the masts again.

He was not a seaman, not a veteran boater. But he had good common sense, he told himself. And for Alexis's peace of mind he did not want to seem flustered.

"Grab a mast and hang on," he shouted to Alexis.

"I already have, for God's sake," Alexis shouted back.

"I know," said Sid. "What I mean is hang on tighter. We're about to do a turn."

Sid had taken the *Marie Celeste*'s tiller firmly into both hands as soon as it had become obvious that no amount of shouting and shaking of fists was going to make the *Panama Banana* slow down, goddamn it. And if the *Marie Celeste*, now exceeding its maximum safe speed by a factor of maybe ten, kept pitching and yawing this way, it was going to go down anyway. Yes, he had a plan, but first he said a small prayer for half rotted-out samson posts, a prayer that said, "Please, whoever you are, make it break off—and make it break off *now*." Then did he swing the tiller hard to port, which caused the *Marie Celeste* to wildly careen hard to starboard.

It seemed the boat was going to capsize by the bows and get pulled along as it lay on its side like a fallen barn dragged away by horsemen. But, Eureka—it worked. The braking force of the turn, the sudden strain on the tug's towline—snap, crack, zing. Some pieces of deck went with it, along with chunks of the deck support—but there it went, the samson post, what was left of it, now left to dangle and skip along the water as the tug *Panama Banana* continued its mad dash to make the bridge in time.

To fully understand the turn of events here, the change in mode of Sid and Alexis's lifestyle as it chanced to evolve that day, we must do an instant playback, to show that more than just samson post sheered. Indeed, to the sickening sound of wood tearing away from wood, the post parted company with its supporting members, sheered through rotted deck and scantlings, and then gave such a jolt to the stem post, before breaking off at the top, that the already none-too-sturdy bow planks gaped open and took in water that came into the hull in a torrent.

For a moment there—well, as Alexis said to Sid, "After all this we're going down anyway?"

But Farley's Slough, as fate would have it (not to mention that Alexis had quickly gone down below to survey the extent of the damage to the bows), was not to have its piece of cake (chocolate, orange-vanilla?) and eat it too that day. Alexis was able to report that the gaps in the bow were just above waterline, so that when the boat's forward motion had subsided, everything seemed okay.

The bilges and floorboards were awash, the stuffing box was leaking worse than ever, so that a little stream, like that from a hole in an old garden hose, was seen to be shooting out of it. The thing now, as Sid advised, was not to rock the boat too much.

He had inadvertently discovered the wisdom of this by his having leaned over the starboard rail to peer down and see whether damage had been done to the hull's planking amidships. As he leaned, the boat leaned. Water came rushing in through gaps in the starboard bow. Each time he and Alexis went walking on deck, inspecting this and that for damage, the boat leaned and wallowed and seemed about to take the final gulp of water that would scuttle it for sure.

The best thing to do, it was decided, was to have Alexis sit on the starboard rail at just about midships, and Sid on the port rail at just about midships there, too, after making a careful adjustment in consideration of their different weights. And so there they sat, port and starboard, the *Marie Celeste* even then in precarious balance—a creaking teeter-totter in an unlikely aquatic setting, ready to go either way if so much as a breeze came up.

"What do we do now?" said Alexis.

"Stay put and hope help comes along," said Sid.

Captain Wally of the *Panama Banana* would ascribe the events that followed to Kismet—a miracle brought on by a state of heightened awareness, a good Thai stick before breakfast. He knew something was wrong back there, certainly. First the tug seemed to want to lurch sharply to port, and then—when finally the samson did break off—it surged ahead at an unheard of speed of 14 knots.

It was Samantha who ran aft to quickly look out the window. The roller shade stuck, but that didn't stop her. She yanked it off the hooks—and, "Good, God A'mighty!" she shouted back at Wally, "If you don't get your ass out of the tow job business, I'm leaving you."

Captain Wally ran back to the window to see for himself. He hit himself on the side of the head with a fist. "Look at that mother," he told Samantha. "Is it sinking? Can you tell?"

He ran back to the pilothouse, grabbed the wheel, and spun the tug sharply to starboard, in a violent one-eighty that sent the crew tumbling into the pilothouse's port wall. "Hey," shouted Wally, "you dip-shits, stand up straight. Get your asses in gear. There's two Billy pumps down below. Go find one."

Holding the speed at 14 knots, worried sick that the diesel's pistons were going to pound the driveshaft right out the bottom, Captain Wally steered straight for the wallowing *Marie Celeste*. When the tug came to a distance of about 50 yards from it, he slammed the diesel into reverse.

The screw churned and thrashed like a giant auger that had to suck up mud and debris from the slough's bottom to get a solid hold on something to stop the tug's forward motion. But stop it did, and then Captain Wally, easy-like, very easy-like, put the screw in forward. Thum-thum, thum-thum, slow and easy, the screw turning so slowly it looked like it would stop dead every time one of the big blades rose to the water's surface and then plunged back down again with the seemingly effortless force of its own weight.

Thum, thum, thum, it went, an easy yard at a time, until Captain Wally had brought the *Panama Banana*, with such gentle expertise as surprised even Samantha, to within a foot of the *Marie Celeste*'s port rail, so that the whole stoned and contrite crew, and Samantha, who carried a Billy pump under an arm, were able to quickly cast out lines, secure one vessel to the other, and then leap aboard to the rescue.

To everyone's surprise, both Billy pumps worked. Their motors began to purr at speed at a single pull of the cords. Even their hoses and valves were clear, so that soon were the *Marie Celeste*'s bilges pumped out to the point that the boat gained the buoyancy necessary to lift the ruptured bows safely above the surface of Farley's Slough for the tow back to Aldo's, alas. It was Sid and Alexis's decision not to be towed on down to the city to fix the leaking stuffing box that might rightly be charged with having been responsible for so much of what had turned out badly that day. To the kneebone is connected the thighbone, to the thighbone, the. . . . The *Marie Celeste* would not have made it there, anyway. An old, wood classic fix'er-upper to the last.

The story doesn't end here, however. Thank God, it doesn't end here, or else we'd all be in trouble. We might get the wrong idea about classic fix'er-uppers. We need to crank up the time frame adjustments in our sequence and, quick, show what has come to pass three years after the Farley's Slough disaster. Sid and Alexis, we shall see, have made certain adjustments in their lives.

For one thing, they are calling Aldo's positively home now. And the *Marie Celeste*—well, it is still there at its slip just off the point, and it is afloat. The gaping holes in the upper portion of the bows have long been plugged with cement, though from a distance the result of this is not easily noticed. Sid and Alexis went to some effort to "mold it in." The hull's original classic lines are classic still, if in an original way that includes both the cement and another of Aldos' specials—black epoxy paint, 10 percent off.

As for the leaking stuffing box, well, Captain Wally returned the entire $150 paid for the tow job, which Sid, in turn, reinvested in part in quarts of quick-fix Gluvit. That very next weekend following the Farley's Slough business, Captain Wally and Crew showed Sid and Alexis how to beach the *Marie Celeste* between the tides, and the tug's crew went at it two days straight with caulking guns, while Captain Wally fixed the stuffing box for all time by pumping it full of epoxy.

The old Studebaker engine, rusty and frozen up in the cylinders, is still there, poking into the main saloon from out of the dark hole just under the *Marie Celeste*'s stern sheets. Sid has covered it over, however, with wood. It now has a pine plank top that makes a nice combination bar and service table, being located next to the galley. The sides of the box Alexis covered with cedar shingles neatly cut to a Victorian scallop pattern. Much of the redecorated interior of the *Marie Celeste* is like this—sort of funk mountain chalet, but not so overwhelming as to intrude upon altogether a general ambience of good, salty boatiness. There's a chiming ship's clock and matching brass barometer, for example, mounted not far from a full-size, four-burner, cast-iron cooking and heating stove that used to be Alexis's grandmother's. The stove is great on long, wet winter nights. Sid uses coal, which burns long and hot. Sacks of it are stored in what once was the after anchor locker.

When it rains, the decks don't leak anymore, the bunks are cozy and warm, and now are there three bunks that are permanently being occupied. "Sweet Pea," they've nicknamed her, though the given name of the now two-year-old addition to the *Marie Celeste* household is Sue. As a matter of fact, it was when Sue appeared that Sid built a raised shingle roof over "the whole damned deck," as he was happy to show his friend the veteran boating man from the city, when one day he came to visit.

Certainly the *Marie Celeste* now bore no resemblance to his own restored wood classic. The shingle roof over Sid's deck, propped on two-by-fours—that he found most disappointing. On his own boat, the teak decks had been restored to original perfection. On Monday mornings, after a hard weekend's sail, the hired boy first thing scrubbed down the decks with Teak Brite Powder Cleaner. Those were standing orders. But here, at Sid's "place," as it had become—"Jesus, you just don't do this to a boat," he thought privately.

But to Sid he said, congenially, "What you've got yourself here, partner, is a country cabin up Farley's Slough." His nose twitched. He wasn't sure he had said the right thing.

It hadn't started out to be this way, of course. As a matter of fact, embedded in clear epoxy on the top of the folding table in the main saloon is the British Admiralty chart of Bora Bora that Sid years ago bought for a dollar at the nautical flea market.

"So what the hell," Sid tells the skeptical boating friend who rubs his nose with the back of his hand. "Now I sit drinking coffee with my ass at Aldo's and my feet propped on Bora Bora. When the wind blows, the boat rocks. When it rains, hell, we light up the stove, fix a hot buttered rum, and . . . ."

"Come on now, I bet you think we're nuts," Alexis breaks in to tell the boating friend. She says this with such obvious pride that, when he winces his nose to indicate both agreement and disgust, he thinks better of it and scratches his head to show at least a willingness to give the matter thought.

Sue–Sweet Pea, wearing an orange life vest several sizes too large (at night and during naps, she sleeps with it clutched to her as if it were a favorite doll), tugs at her mother's dress and gives the veteran boating man a dirty look and a sneer. "I like the boat, Mommy. If we lived in a house, we wouldn't be here," she says.

"Damned right," says Sid. "And this one's paid for. Not just anybody can say that. Aldo never did find the pink slip. But that's okay. Nobody's ever come asking."

Well, now, that's certainly one way of fixing up an old wood classic that never wanted to get fixed up in **the** first place.

Chapter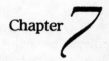

Secret and Sublime

Potent Quotes

*"I have some idea how to do it, the mechanical part. I
figure I can figure it out, or what I can't figure on my own
I can cookbook together . . . . "*

John Jerome
Truck

*"Let a man of spirit venture where he pleases
and never tip his gold cup empty toward the moon."*

Lì Po

*"Had the Venus de Milo been cast in fiberglass, God forbid,
her chief claims to posterity would be not her richly tactile
flow and ebb of female indentations (I must admit to a
hearty grasping on several occasions while passing), but in
the manufacturer's claim that, dropped off a cliff at 2,000
feet, the heavenly lady suffered no more damage than was
easily repaired with a ready application of gel-coat. She
would have come bouncing at us through the ages like
next year's model of a Brunswick bowling ball. Now, can a
fiberglass boat be any different, Gentlemen?"*

Smasden Kosinski, KMT,
Ninth Annual Address
Friends of Snow Planet
Ski Touring & Small Boat
Cruising Society

BOAT MADE OF fiberglass, as is Alice and Stanley's, certainly won't have the maintenance problems that Sid and Alexis had. As Richard Henderson, in his excellent book *Sea Sense*, tells us, one of the indeed great advantages of fiberglass is its "freedom from corrosion and rot, and destruction from worms." Worms simply have no taste for fiberglass, and goats are sooner to eat plastic bowling balls than will rot and corrosion get the best of fiberglass.

Alice, in the letter we left off with a while back, says: "When first we considered buying our boat, Stanley and I weren't too keen on fiberglass. We really liked the design of the boat, and it wasn't that we had any doubts about the structural integrity of the stuff. Did you know my father, when he died, was buried in a fiberglass coffin?

"Everyone who went by at the funeral parlour thumped on it—you know, little pats and thumps of the hand—to see what it was like. My uncle George said it was a great idea but that this one looked like my father had died in the bathtub and they couldn't get him out of it, so, he, my uncle George, was going to wait till the new models came out before buying one. My aunt Terese, Uncle George's wife, she said . . . . "

Yes, Alice, you told me that story. Please, stick to the storyline. We're sailing for the sun, remember? Get thee to the bosom of the sea?

"Matters of the heart—that's what gives us a mystique about living," she goes on finally. "The feel of wood, for instance, when you run your hand along the top of a beautifully polished table of pine or oak or teak. There's a feeling of union with the forest, with other hands that have made the table. The same with a beautifully made wood boat— you get the feeling there's something *there* there." Alice, if you're going to be bringing Gertrude Stein into the mishmash, a lot of us are going to be taking Li Po's advice and getting on our way in the very first boat we can get our hands on. What— you really wished you'd bought a wood boat?

"My God," Alice finally gets around to say, "when first we bought the boat it was fitted out like an el-cheapo Travelodge down below, not to mention what the former owners had done to it."

Stanley and Alice's, it should be said, is a Sixties model, a decade in fiberglass construction when the manufacturers were making interiors to resemble mini garden condos in Southern California beach towns.

As Alice says of theirs, however, "The designers went more the Travelodge route, with a little condo mixed in to make it more homey, I'm sure." Marketing directors were in those days prepped on demographic studies that showed that wives were too frequently having the last say: the husband wants the boat because it sails well, but the wife says no, there's no place to fix a decent meal.

Armed with carpet and fabric samples, the marketing men now were putting in color-coordinated settees and curtains, stoves with ovens, easy-to-clean vinyl cushions, full-service kitchen arrangements. In Alice's boat, to the back of a pullman-kitchen-size formica countertop (a tiny stainless steel sink, scarcely capable of containing four tea cups, confirmed the scaled-down, condo-kitchen nature of the arrangement) was a handy cupboard. "Cute," said Alice, "—but condos don't heel over when the wind blows. The good ones don't, anyway."

When their boat was on the starboard tack, for instance, the dishes in the cupboard, along with the salt and pepper shakers, the catsup bottle and the Ajax can—you didn't dare open the sliding plastic panels just then. "We didn't do it a second time, I mean," said Alice. She first thing tore out *that* whole business.

The sink, for instance, was replaced with a wood bucket—a Japanese soy sauce tub bought at a flea market—which was large enough that Alice could take it out to the cockpit and do the laundry outdoors. But this was just the beginning of what was to become a fullscale and very frustrating interior redevelopment project. In the interim, said Alice, "The wood soy sauce bucket, it had that venerable patina that wood gets with age. The soy sauce gave it a nice patina, too. It was the only thing in the boat at that time that had soul. The only thing Stanley and I had to go on then was the sheer faith that if we kept on stripping the crap away, eventually we would get down to the boat's true self. Like stripping away veils to find the Buddha nature of it."

Two months went by, two months of consternating peeling, chipping, and ripping away at everything the manufacturer's marketing people had put in down below and which the former owners, man and wife, had embellished in kind. Most notable of the wife's efforts, to be sure, was the Louisa Mae wallpaper (strawberry pink, vertical stripes with geranium motif, painted over with epoxy varnish to hold down the mildew, it appeared) plastered to all three walls of the boat's tiny head—or "Powder Room," as said the brass sign plate affixed to the door's outside.

The powder room's fourth closure was of course the door, which was slightly warped and had to be banged once, twice, three times before finally the latch caught and it shut.

To the door, on the commode side, was fastened the antique brass toilet roll holder that struck Stanley square on the chin the first time he shut the door by reaching out to grab it while sitting in there. That he ripped out by the screws instantly. But the wallpaper—that took most of two days of unrelenting applications of acetone, scraping, peeling, wire brushing.

Blow torches were used to peel away sheets of eternally glued formica, frustrating work at best, as often splintered layers of cheap plywood remained glued no matter and had to be wrenched away, screaming, from countertops and cabinet sides. And so the cheap plywood cabinetry, wherever that was found—that went out to the dumpster too, along with the settee (table, slide-in seats, vinyl upholstery, the works), bunk supports, and powder room door, until all that remained of the old, garden condo ticky-tacky, was the fading polyvinyl smile of a plucked Cheshire Cat, the former owners' *His-N-Hers Too* glued in a single, crinkle-free sheet across the boat's otherwise graceful transom. But then, records Alice, a rather disconcerting thing happened.

"Just standing there, taking it all in," said Alice, "was like scratching your fingernails up and down it. Shit, we were down to raw fiberglass." Late one night, in the light of a full moon coming in through the opened forward hatch, a morbid curiosity made Alice get out of bed and do just that, scratch the wall in the former powder room, where the Louisa Mae wallpaper had been. Chalky white dust, bits of glass fiber gathered under her fingernails. The sound of it sent Stanley bursting out of his sleeping bag. Worse, now that he was fully awake on this terrible night of realization, he itched so bad he yelled about it. Invisible strands of fiber, like particles of glass wool, clung to his pubic hairs, the hair on his chest, the back of his neck.

"Li Po would have been out of his mind with this stuff," said Alice. "Itch, itch, we nearly died."

Yes, Alice, Captain Nemo would have been pretty burned up about this too. It would not have suited his great sense of dignity. And what would Gertrude Stein say—fiberglass is fiberglass and there isn't a goddamned thing you can do about it, a goddamned thing you can do about it?

Chapter

Master Wu Takes a Lady Friend
Zen Boating

Potent Quotes

"He was opposed to busybody-like interference with the affairs and thoughts of others and regarded an official career under prevailing conditions both useless to the community and dangerous to oneself. But little is known of Yang Chu, one of the founding fathers of Taoism. . ."

John Blofeld,
The Secret and Sublime

"I am not what you call a civilized man. I have done with society entirely, for reasons which I alone have the right of appreciating. You have come to trouble my existence."

Captain Nemo,*
Twenty Thousand Leagues Under
The Sea

---

*As well as being omen spelled backward, the name Nemo reads in Latin to mean "the nameless one." A namelessly similar phrase is used by old-time Taoists to characterize not only the elusive Yang Chu, but also certain "Taoist renegade types" who "quit hard times at home by taking to the sea in boats." They had their reasons.

ND SO IN THE interim of seeking the boat's Buddha nature from pure scratch," Alice tells us in her letter, "—well, we sat, we thought, we fretted.

"It was like trying to think of something clever to do with an old refrigerator that has been sitting around too long in the backyard. If you make a planter out of it, a file cabinet, paint it up to be an *objet d'art*—I dunno, that's what we were trying to figure out."

Still, there had to be some saving grace, a spark somewhere, she told herself day after day—even if she had to arrive at the nature of this in her own peculiar way, as she put it. Actually, she did get a little peculiar after a while. She and Stanley had got to grousing. Stanley was talking of selling the boat.

She took to thoroughly memorizing and then muttering to herself the phrase, "Fiberglass construction has many advantages of compressive and tensile strength, and freedom from corrosion and rot, and destruction from worms." It was the phrase she had acquired from Richard Henderson's good book *Sea Sense*.

She got to the point she even began to dance to the phrase when during the day she chanted it over and over again—little tapping steps that took their rhythm from the placement of the commas. But nothing came of it, she reports.

About this time, was it, that Alice got into the habit of wandering away from the boat during the day. Mostly, she took the bus to town and hung out at Howie Adam's Used Books, it was called, where she browsed high racks made of old two-by-fours and bins made of old cardboard boxes. There she flipped through well-thumbed back issues of *Better Homes and Gardens*, of all things, *Ladies Home Journal, Sunset, Do-It-Yourself Patio Construction,* the sailing buff magazines *Rudder* and *Motorboat & Sailing, The Winnebago Newsletter, Playgirl.* But there was no inspiration here, either, she concluded, that didn't offer more of the same kind of formica-condo-polyvinyl-Winnebago-Travelodge-Bauhaus-Art Deco schmaltz that had been torn out of the boat in the first place. "Crappo," she said.

The only article she found of interest, in fact, was toward the front of a back issue of a women's magazine and which promised in the title page full pictorial instruction on "how to teach your man the oral arts that really turn a woman on." But what the how-to picture pages promised—someone before her, damn it, had torn that out of the magazine.

Then, one day when her frustrations ran so high it made her left eye twitch, Alice stumbled onto something big, way in the back of Howie's Used Books. "It wasn't like I heard a small voice," she would later try to explain. "But something sure as hell said, 'Hi, there.'" She found herself suddenly stopping in the aisle to look up at a tall shelf marked "Cookbooks, Chinese: Cantonese, Szechwan, Hunan."

Instinctively, she guessed it was, Alice reached up to bring down what was apparently a coffee table picture book that bore on the spine of the cover the title *From Far Away Provinces of Hunan—Hot and Spicy*. That must have been it, she would later conclude—the hot and spicy part. But what she found in hand that day, after reaching high on tiptoes to bring it down, was not the book she had reached for.

"My God," said Alice after a few moments of rapidly turning pages and scanning chapter titles and snatches of passages. She dug into the pockets of her jeans, found the money (two seventy-five plus tax), quickly bought the book, went to the park across the street, sat under a large bull pine that kept dropping bits of resin into her hair, and read the thing from cover to cover.

The book finished, her hair sticky with bull pine drippings, Alice caught the first bus to the marina, rushed out to the docks when she got there and ran to the boat to tell Stanley.

She found him fast asleep in the sun, as was his way these difficult days, his head propped on one of several mildewed kapok life vests he had late that morning brought up on deck to dry. He was snoring in fits and starts.

"Stanley, are you awake?" she said.

"No," said Stanley.

"Well, when you do wake up, I want you to read this book," said Alice. "Start at about page ten, that's the best chapter—'Master Wu Takes a Lady Friend Zen Boating.' I'm going below and get started on this."

When she saw Stanley sitting up and holding the book as though he were going to read it, Alice quickly vanished. She didn't want to have to explain anything just now—just go and do it.

As he began to look over the book, the first thing that struck Stanley was that the title was stuffy, the author's name more so.

But what, he thought, can you expect of a little red book privately printed, it was indicated, by one Sir Anton Ritter-LaRue, KMT, Ret., Formerly of Her Majesty's Stationery Office, Hong Kong. Still, thought Stanley, there was something intriguing about it. The picture on the cover, for instance. This depicted a shifty-eyed Chinese with a markedly bulbous nose.

Under the picture, it said "Master Wu, Monk, Pirate, Poet, Inventor—First of International Men to Flourish in 7th Century China." "That nose," thought Stanley—"he must have been into booze."

Stanley turned back the cover, quickly scanned the chapter titles and turned to page 18, it turned out to be, where began the chapter "Master Wu Takes a Lady Friend Zen Boating," just as Alice had told him. And then was it puzzlingly subtitled, he noticed, "And Thus Does Fiberglass in History Take a Marvelous Turn: A Mystique Before Our Time."

"Our story begins," Stanley was trying to read as the boat rocked and down below the radio blared (Alice was down there dancing to the music), "in Hong Kong, 1979, with the discovery of a Chinese historical document linking one Wu the Wayward with what at first glance appears a mere band of sleazy Oriental pirates, the terror of the river Yangtze. . . ."

Chapter 9

When a Bear Takes a Moon Cake Sailing, God Knows but What They Stop along the Way and Poach a Fat Fish

Potent Quote

"For a day and a night the shark swam with the boat. The oarsmen kept their stroke, paying it little attention.

"A week out they spoke the Canadian schooner Jessie *bound to New York with lumber.*

"'Come alongside,' hailed the captain of the Jessie. *'We'll take you aboard.'*

"'Thanks,' Samuelson replied, 'but we're on a voyage.'"

Charles A. Borden
Sea Quest

"WE HAVE NO WAY of knowing whether the peculiar fellow's name of Wu the Wayward was conferred by himself or heaped upon him by his many official detractors, but we do know," the book's author somewhat stuffily went on, "that his refusal to pay the customary boat taxes and secure the required boating operator's permit got him in ill favor with the government of the day.

"He made his position known on the signal occasion of throwing the Emperor's chief tax collector over the rail of his sumptuous seagoing junk, the *Lu Pan*, a large river vessel of the crooked-stern variety much used in negotiating treacherous Yangtze rapids. The splash of the tax man's going over the rail was heard all over the realm, and the Emperor was further put into a classic Chinese tizzy by Wu's having penned strong words on the seat of the tax man's white silk pants. 'Bears,' had written Wu with exquisite strokes of a fine-pointed brush laden with purple ink, 'don't have government. Neither do the fish of the sea. We all of us manage quite nicely, thank you.' The tax man went straight to the Emperor, to be sure, causing Wu to become a much-wanted fellow. What happened next, however—well, only by the most careful translation of a reliable ancient source are we properly able to reconstruct the true story without damaging the legend.

"Indeed," Stanley went on to read, "it was Wu's way to have fled the land by boat, on the premise that prevailing conditions on land were not to his liking in any event. He rather hurried away to sea with permanent residence there in mind—and what a marvelously elusive old boy he was.

"Not only had the Emperor put a price on this man's head, a heavily armed fleet was sent in close pursuit as Wu set sail down the turbulent Yangtze, himself in pursuit of the open sea.

"It is from the Emperor we get it that Wu was promptly brought to bay just east of Soochow, which is as far as he is supposed to have gotten from the mouth of the Yangtze. Fire arrows and buckets of burning tar launched from the naval force's catapults, the citizens of the celestial realm are informed, put a quick end to 'one who would dare rebel.'"

"Shit," thought Stanley. "It's those tubby Chinese junks. Wu—if he had any brains—would have had a faster boat." To that extent, Wu's tale up to now was disappointing to Stanley.

"But, ah," Sir Anton happily reveals, "what we have here is the case of high government's wanting the people to think one thing when quite something else has taken place. Matter of fact, they never so much as got their hands on the old boy's coattails.

"Just as Wu is cornered east of Soochow, as is thus far factually reported, he is seen by nearby simple fisherfolk to perform a masterful leap from off the bow of the burning *Lu Pan*, the hems of his pirate's finery aflap. Wouldn't you know it, it is at the instant of Wu's splashing into the murky waters of the Yellow Sea that a typically mythic Chinese event takes place. The junk *Lu Pan* is seen to grow wings, rather like those of a great Chinese dragon. The vessel is last seen winging its way into the northern heavens.

"Rather than their having been made to cower at the sight of Wu's head on a pole by way of public example, indeed has it been the taxpayers' pleasure to make of Wu an exemplary pirate-God—immortals ensconced in the sea are quite beyond the long arm of the tax collector, you see. Or so we are left to account for the happy persistence of the legend to this day."

"For chrissake," Stanley at this point says aloud, "—so what actually happened to the guy?"

Stanley, like the Emperor's dogged and dogging naval forces, resolutely reads on, while in the back of his mind he's wondering what was it in this book that got Alice so excited. And what the hell is she doing down there? The radio blares, the boat is shaking—and fresh paint, is that what he smells?

Well, the book is getting pretty damned exciting at this point, he can see. Wu the Wayward is just now seen to pop up on "a mysterious island in Thailand, where he is known to have hung out with a band of renegade Zen-Taoist-Buddhist types, a lot of them magicians, most of them rascals, and all, to the core, boat bums. For Wu, this is home, but the Emperor's men are well aware of this. He will quickly have to get along on his way.

"What he does is build a boat, which is a much scaled-down version of his beloved *Lu Pan*, really, the smaller boat premised on his notion, wisely taken, that 'one small mackerel slips easily through the net set to catch but a prized halibut.'"

Now comes the revelation that Sir Anton seems to have so doggedly set Stanley up for—or apparently, as it stands if we are to judge by the holy-cow look of amazement on Stanley's face as he reads the stuff. Says Sir Anton: "Wu's tiny vessel of ultimate escape and disbursement is but 27 feet long and made of alternating layers of specially woven silk melded together by a remarkably resilient glue of some sort developed and extensively tested beforehand by some of Wu's alchemist boat bum cohorts. So light a boat, this turns out to be, quite sea-capable obviously, and in appearance it is rather like a fine piece of Oriental lacquerware that has the additional advantage of its being all but shatterproof, a feature that Wu's further adventuring will much require. Did the good Captain Nemo, with that tinker-toy contraption of his, ever have so practical a vessel? We rather think not."

"Well, I'll be goddamned," says Stanley. Or, as Sir Anton has said before him, we know, and perhaps in anticipation of Stanley's selfsame thought, "And thus does fiberglass in history take a marvelous turn . . . . " Sir Anton, however, at risk of overburdening his already laden story line, does not leave it at that.

"Departing the mysterious island, way back in the 7th century, in this remarkably advanced boat of his, Wu sails west, in the general direction of Africa, setting a crinkum-crankum course that soon has his sailing companion wondering aloud exactly what is Wu's master plan.

"Indeed, he commemorates the start of this apparently mindless voyage by dashing off a poem. 'East, West, all around— / who's to say, who's to know? / My golden wine cup is filled to the brim. / I play my bamboo flute, toot, toot. / If on the morrow I catch a fat tuna— / is it not the gods who bade me take my fishing pole?'"

Still, we are left to wonder what is the saving grace, the

eminent confirmation of purpose in his life, now that Wu has this great little boat of his—and, really, now, is the boat all that it is cracked up to be?

Off the coast of Sumatra ("Jesus," Stanley whistles through his teeth, "this is great stuff"), is there the predictable encounter with pirates. Actually was it Wu who blundered into them, near the island land of Sinabang, it is believed to be, early one morning when minding his fishing pole and not looking around to see who had come up from behind. "He is instantly alerted, at the last possible moment, by a pirate's arrow shot through the sleeve of his robe as he is pulling in a breakfast fish."

On his toes now, at last—indeed is it Wu's boat of innovative design that saves the day! The all-new *Lu Pan*'s "sailplan and rigging, its sleek underwater profile and ballasted keel, the highly responsive skeg rudder so ahead of its time—all enable Wu to masterfully sail upwind at speed. Baffled, outrun, made fools of just when sure the second arrow would get him, the Sumatran pirates gave up the chase, leaving Wu, in short while, to leisurely fix his fish for breakfast."

Indeed, so confident was Wu of the *Lu Pan*'s ability to blithely outrun the pirate's old-fashioned wood junks, all the while of the chase did he have his sailing companion down below heating bottles of rice wine, one after the other, in the ceramic charcoal stove that is the heart of the *Lu Pan*'s "simple but highly functional and delightfully well-appointed galley," Sir Anton tells us.*

Indeed, Sir Anton shows Wu's having extended his love of the "well-appointed galley," in this instance, to include the cook—the sailing companion but briefly mentioned early on. This would be Moon Cake, a longterm young woman friend of

---

*As for Wu's obviously superior and advanced sailplan, Sir Anton's depiction of it gives us a greatly simplified junk rig, with single bamboo mast and what in our time has come to be known as the modern Chinese lug rig. That Wu's version of the same would have produced a quite able vessel is demonstrated by the Englishman H. G. Hasler's 25-foot folkboat, Jester, a single-masted Chinese lug rig that has several times had him well in front in the Singlehanded Transatlantic race.

Wu's from a lovely island off Thailand. For "various good reasons," we are told, she shares Wu's love of the boating life—though she is not always certain of where it is going to take them. "She was game if he was," Sir Anton explains the matter, "Wu did not resist. Neither had he talked her into this. We get a picture of a mutually shared flair for the crinkum-crankum uncertainties of the boating life."

It is shortly after Wu has so deftly evaded the pirates, Stanley reads on with measurably growing interest, "that the victor's jade spear rises to the occasion as Moon Cake, her skirts up and the fire up in the galley stove, heats yet another bottle of tasty rice wine and puts the breakfast fish (a plump bonita) to poach in a small but efficient cast-iron wok especially designed by Wu for use aboard a small vessel of this type.

"Shortly, the poaching fish is turned to its other side as indeed Moon Cake expertly works the ladle and Wu, who is depicted standing close behind her, a merry cup of wine in hand, expertly pleasures Moon Cake, the result of which, all in all, has caused a most lascivious look of pleasure to appear on both their faces."

Sir Anton, Stanley is becoming impatiently aware, further describes the *Lu Pan* cook-aboard scene in terms to bring home his earlier design assessment of the boat's being remarkably advanced for its time—and, yes, in this regard much like a fine piece of Oriental lacquerware. "Black on the inside, mandarin red on the outside, exquisitely furnished with simple but highly functional elegance—an elegance enhanced by the complete lack of pseudo-boating bric-a-brac and the thorough installation of simple, commonsensical creature comforts. In a word, Zen."

Sir Anton doggedly goes on from there, painting of the boat's interior a scene which he describes as down-home splendor, with most of the necessary items and accoutrements having been purchased by Wu, on last moment's notice, at an oriental flea market in Thailand.

"There are thick, warm quilts for the single doublebunk in the forepeak (used but nice quilts), paper candle lanterns strung here and there, where they provide either the most romantic or most practical effect (the practical lantern is in the galley), wicker and brass-trim chests pleasantly stuffed with clothes and spare boat parts (plus a plentiful supply of sandlewood joss sticks for both the luck and the pleasing aroma these give), many, many bottles and jugs of rice wine, and then here and there, again, various wall hangings and decorative items of many splendid colors. Rather than drab, as we might think, the ebony black walls and bulkheads through and through, in combination with the candle lanterns, warmly enhance the interior coloration, the overall charisma of it being somewhat that of a Finnish country inn and crafts shop run by Chinese and lighted with candles in wintertime."

Suddenly did it dawn on Stanley. A Finnish inn and crafts shop? A fine piece of Oriental lacquerware? Wasn't that fresh paint he smelled a while back?

To be sure, Alice, down below, goes on painting just as Stanley is seen to tentatively poke his head down the main hatch to see what's up down there. Alice is stark naked? There's a big splotch of ebony black paint on her behind?

Alice is charmingly bent over, her back to Stanley, as she reaches down to paint beneath a strip of fiberglass left from having torn the old bunks out of the forepeak and which she plans to use for supports for the bed arrangements she has in mind.

"Black?" says Stanley. "She's painting the whole goddamned inside of the boat black?"

Alice has turned off the radio. She has lots to think about now that she has decided that the paint is exactly right. Hadn't she seen a quilt at the flea market last Sunday? Have they anything to swap for it? Lanterns from Japan Town in San Francisco? Where was the little shop in Chinatown where she saw the charcoal wok stove that was exactly the right size for in the galley?

Still, for all her concentration on all these important little details, she is able to paint and sing at the same time.

"East, West, all around," she sings. "I play my flute, toot, toot. Who's to say, who's to know? Toot, toot . . . . Hell, I can't remember the rest of it."

"Holy Jesus smuckers," shouts Stanley. "Holy Jesus smuckers."

Captain Nemo, it is Stanley's strong opinion at the moment, would sure as hell feel right about blowing his cork about this—and it wouldn't be just Holy Jesus smuckers. He'd blow the whole thing right out of the goddamned water.

But then Stanley is no more Captain Nemo than he is Lewis Carroll (Li Po? Gertrude Stein?).

Have things got out of hand here? It has been the history of boating that often things do in the end.

Chapter 10

Christmas upon the Waters and How a Couple of Mugs Made Hay of It

Potent Quotes

". . . Self-sufficiency, for our time a major form of freedom. . . . And freedom as it expresses itself in and through the creative act is its object. There is finally no 'truth,' just this sense of freedom. And love is the pleasure of freedom."

Alfred Kazin,
Bright Book of Freedom

"I had awakened at five and decided to fish for a few hours. I rowed the dinghy out to the boat on that lovely foggy morning and then headed around my side of Martha's Vineyard into the heavy waters of West Chop. Up toward Lake Tashmoo I found the quiet rip where the flounders had been running, put out two lines, and made myself some coffee. I am always child-happy when I am alone in a boat. . . . "

Lillian Hellman,
Pentimento

*T*IME AND TIME AGAIN has the history of boating, like waves striking the shore time and time again, shown itself to be deeply imbued with a hidden sense of purpose—and you just have to get your feet wet to find out what that is.

"Actually, Stanley got to kind of like the black paint when I showed him that I knew what to do to set it off with richly textured whites (fluffy throw pillows on the double berth in the forepeak, for instance), golds and reds and blues (the quilt—which I ended up having to make because the one I found in the store that was exactly right was too damned expensive), and then a radiant mix of sort of grape-gold-silver (as in the washable bathroom rugs I cut up to make carpeting—stuff that felt good on bare feet).

"At night, when I've lit the Japanese candle lanterns, it all comes together like a lighted painting hung on a wall in a very dark room. Out of darkness comes color, against a world that is turning a buff-gray like the leaves of trees that have been standing along a highway. Color is life against drab shapes that have no peace and freedom to them.

"We both agreed heartily that Mandarin red, lightened up a bit to resemble a good, ripe Mexican chili pepper, was just the right sauce to paint the hull with, and that's what Stanley did. For one thing, he prefers working outside, in the fresh air, and so any decorating he wanted to do, that's where he did it."

As we get it from Alice, Stanley likes to get into the paint from time to time himself, and he had, to be sure, painted the hull of the *Lu Pan* a mighty chili pepper Mandarin red, which was a success to the extent that the boat did seem to suggest, to anyone with a mind for it, its being made of anything but drab petrochemical goop dipped out of barrels. It certainly bore no resemblance to the fiberglass crate that Alice's father was put to eternal rest in.

It had been the way of Wu the Wayward, who can be blamed for much of the inspiration that went into Alice and Stanley's modest re-creation, to resort to alchemy and other off-color arts to get his boat looking the way it did.

The results of that fixing-up project ran more than skin deep, to produce a boat of immortal qualities—one that would sail through life and history for so long as the owner had the patience for it. Actually, and as Sir Anton Ritter-LaRue tells us in his book, Wu, along with Moon Cake, sailed immortally on after the run-in with the pirates of Sinabang, but did, in 1805, experience what appears to have been a major setback.

Tooting around, as he did, from one sea to the next, never quite sure where he was bound or why, and with no mind to bother himself with charts and plans and such, he inadvertently sailed into the midst of the Battle of Trafalgar. Nelson was there in force giving Napoleon's fleet hell. Cannonballs flew every which way for miles around. Wu's tiny boat, while he and Moon Cake were apparently down below poaching a nice breakfast fish, caught a very large stray one.

"It shatters me miserably," writes Sir Anton, "to think that a cheap shot of fickle fate's would have such a fine little boat as this snuffed like a candle. Wu, however, did by hook and crook, and God knows what other means, manage to turn up in Florence, Italy, some years later. Jules Verne, who on occasion hung out at the Hotel Oriental there, says Wu and 'a certain Mademoiselle Tourteau de Lune' ran a little imports shop but a short walk from the hotel. One of their hottest selling items, it appears, were miniature replicas of the junk *Lu Pan*. Jules Verne said he bought one of the things.

Alice and Stanley's fixing-up of their *Lu Pan*, as indeed they agreed it should be named, seemed to go on forever. "Months passed like cars moving back and forth in a parking lot that was full-up and with all the meters showing overtime," said Alice. Then one day, finally, Alice stood on the dock in Sausalito watching Stanley parade the thoroughly refurbished *Lu Pan*, with all its apparently odd and eccentric working parts and decorative elements, back and forth for her inspection.

A brisk wind blew. The sky, though gray, had for Stanley the quality of a great, flat stagelight that smelled of a sort of luminous ozone and had the same peculiar freshness that marked the wind. Even the pale green waters of the bay, which here and there showed perfectly white whitecaps, seemed to be of expanded atomic particles freed from gravity's pull by the quality of the light that shone that day. It was to be a magic day, thought Stanley.

Not putting on airs exactly, he was going to be pleased to show of what stuff his newly completed rerigging job was made. But as already Alice saw from the distance and as Stanley knew from having to deal with the damned thing, the staysail that Stanley had mounted behind the jib was shooting back wind and turbulence that made the mainsail flap and flutter in a way that gave the whole rig more the quality of hung laundry, thought Alice, than that of the classy little cutter Stanley had modeled his rig after.*

The sail that was causing most of the trouble, or such trouble as had come to exist at this point, was the used one, from off a vintage catboat, that had to be cut down considerably to make it a staysail and give the boat's rig its cutter nature—and then cut again, and then several times after that, as I recall, to get it right by Stanley's nature.

Back at the dock, Alice had been joined by a gaggle of onlookers, most of whom were friends and acquaintances who lived and berthed at the same yacht harbor in which Stanley and Alice were keeping their boat. And Stanley was damned sure that Alice back there was catching an earful, for he was just now reefing the baggy staysail, which he had to do in the crude but effective fisherman's style, by clumping up the clew portion and putting a couple of turns of line around the ungainly clump to prevent its breaking loose in the wind. Stanley was right, of course: this didn't do much to make his rig a nautical class act, but it did solve the practical problem of the sail's flapping like a canvas bag on a clothesline, as it had.

Alice knew the man standing next to her only by the nicknames given him by the harbor's longterm live-aboard residents, for his penchant for regularly patrolling the docks and giving crisp deliverance of all manner of boating advice.

---

*Actually, this was more something he saw in his head than something he "saw outside of it," Alice tells us. What, a composite of this and that, fixed in his mind's eye like a picture that only a da Vinci could draw and get right? A Mona Lisa boat? Still, Alice assures us, a good portion of Stanley's rig idea came from a very real depiction on page 199 of Richard Henderson's always welcome Sea Sense, a nifty boat, indeed, entitled "A Modern Offshore Cruising Cutter."

Little Nemo, Yachtzy Two-Shoes, Commander Blight, as variously he was called, was the new harbormaster charged with enforcing the new management's extensive list of new regulations. Only this morning had he come down the dock to tell Alice to get her damned laundry out of the rigging.

In her hurry to help Stanley get the boat out of the slip, she had gathered up from off the boom of the mainsail the six pairs of pale blue bikini panties (every last pair that she owned, actually), and then hung them on a line hastily rigged, fore and aft, in the *Lu Pan*'s main saloon. They hung that way still as Stanley put the boat through its paces.

Now, wearing his customary navy blue clipper cap with the embroidered gold bird blap on the visor that conveyed his having official capacity of the probably paramilitary kind, Nemo-Two-Shoes-Bligh trained 7 x 50 binoculars on the *Lu Pan* as it gathered speed about 500 yards off the end of the dock. Thin lips tightened like rubber bands as he caught sight of Stanley's bagged and flopping staysail. Eyes like holes in a sheet of aluminum foil narrowed to become slits in that sheet of foil as he looked upon Stanley and Alice's nautical crumbum paint job.

Alice had to admit to herself that Stanley sure as hell had done a crude job of it. Black pupils, red brows, blazing ochre eyeballs—vivid colors feverishly applied with a warped, long-handled sign painter's brush—both eyes were pretty damned cockeyed, the one of the starboard side being noticeably higher than the one on the port side. Stanley had been in such a hurry to finish the job—and he wasn't going to sail the boat unless they were on it. He had had a strange dream about the need to do that, he had told her.

But now, as freshly she sized them up from the distance, she saw something magical in those eyes. She was having the realization that the eyes reminded her of those of a freshly caught fish looking out of place and supremely dumbfounded as it lay on a butcher's block in a kitchen in the back of a cheap but good Chinese restaurant. But then, flashes of realization, on the way to becoming that definitive *ah-ha* of perfect synthesis and understanding, were known to her to dance about like summer lightning before it knows to hit what it had aimed for—then suddenly fish eyes became chicken eyes staring out of a severed chicken head, and now she knew.

The magic in the boat's eyes came of her realization that Stanley's bad paint-and-brush work had somehow succeeded in melding the boat's disparate design elements in the same way that Chinese cooks, if they're any good, make boiled chicken look and taste like perfectly delicious fried duck. Lightning strokes of a good sharp cleaver (Stanley had had to hack, but still . . .), the choice of a sauce of just the right color (Stanley had had to badly improvise, but not in vain)—and there you have it. Neither cutter nor junk, Alice concluded, the *Lu Pan* was chicken-duck and either you like it or you lump it. That's what she told Commander Push-Foot as he stared at the *Lu Pan* through binoculars. The look of smug satisfaction on his face was that of a veteran sailing man who knows a crappy boat when he sees one, and there was not an argument in the world that was going to change his opinion about this. Already was he telling Alice that Stanley wasn't going to win any races in town with that thing if he didn't know enough to "reef down the main in a wind like *this*, young lady."

Not that a wind of 25 knots or so—and which was gusting up to 5 or 10 knots more that day—is a howling fury. It was that a little less foresail and a reefed main would have taken off much of the wind pressure that was driving under the *Lu Pan*'s lee rail.

True, Little Nemo had found rightful fault, if you want to get technical about it, with Stanley's heeling the boat too far over and thereby losing fine rudder control.

Even as Alice stood there on the dock did the wind gust a good 10 knots. Yachtzy-Two-Shoes' cap blew off and he ran to catch it. Alice, caught by surprise, stumbled back several feet. Her dress blew up.

Of the gaggle of onlookers stationed to catch the *Lu Pan*'s performance, only Sven Lars-Oldegard took his eyes off the now greatly heeled *Lu Pan* to notice, with lurid attention to detail, that the wind had lifted Alice's skirt to indelicately revealing heights. His eyes, for the briefest second allotted, had captured the poetry of what he saw, the glowing picture of which fixed itself in his mind's eye and which for weeks to come he would ever be entitling *Wind in Spanish Moss Blowing Hot Embers.*

Sven moved close to Alice. He made to slip an arm about her waist, and said, "On a windy day like this, how come you don't wear panties? I have seen you wear some nice blue ones." Alice pushed Sven's hand away. The gust of a moment ago had subsided, but now another struck, and Alice crouched and tacked down the hem of her skirt by using both hands to pull it over her knees and cinch it there. Seeing that, imagining chill winds tingling bare embers of squatting spanish moss, Sven felt himself becoming immensely erect. He hitched up his pants to hide it. Oooh-hooh, how the wind blew!

On the boat when the blast hit, Stanley instinctively leaned far to windward as the lee rail buried itself deeper. Green water came rushing over the rail and into the cockpit. The water pulled off one of his shoes as he kicked out to brace himself just as it went rushing out. No matter, thought Stanley—it was just an old moccasin-style deckshoe, the sole of which was coming off. He pulled off the remaining one and flung it in the bay.

The wind (whooooszh), the blobs of salt water striking at his face (smash-splat) as the windward side of the bow shattered (whack-whack) the tops of onrushing white caps, the shock waves (whomp-bang-whomp) coursing up his spine as the boat seemed to want to pound out its undersides—all this was making him giddy, a romantic fool heeling his boat to the limit for the sheer, mad pleasure of it.

Only hours later would he feel pain from the splinter being thrust deeply into the soft underpart of his thumb as the thick, oak tiller clutched in his hand bucked and trembled to the explosion of rushing water that engulfed the rudder at the tiller's other end. It was all he could do to prevent the tiller's breaking free of his grasp.

Both the foresails—the jib and the mule with its reefed clew a big clump—were obscuring his vision. He couldn't see a thing ahead of him, really. But he was more than confident— he was exhilarated by the very idea of it, that the *Lu Pan*, its chili-pepper red sides ablaze, its all-seeing eyes fixed on the path ahead, had acquired a life force of its own that was of a mind, too, that was both his and not his. It had come alive, this boat.

"Blow, ye winds, blow," Stanley shouted. "Smack flat the thick rotundity of the world." If Shakespeare knew to write lines like that, thought Stanley, sure as hell somebody must have taken him sailing at least once in his life.

All who were standing on the dock that day were getting an eyeful, to be sure, and Commander T. Binoculars was first to assess the situation, which he did with great nautical purport. He made a scoffing noise, as if punctuating *fait accompli*, a heavy sentence, indeed, with a well-aimed snort. Give it another hundred yards, he said, and the crum-bum *Lu Pan* was going to hit a boat anchored in the harbor out there.

Sven Lars-Oldegard saw it too and figured Stanley was going to hit the old fishing smack, a decrepit-looking yawl with salmon poles thrust up in its rigging, right smack amidships. He made to put a consoling arm about Alice's shoulder, but thought better of it when she cupped her hands and began to shout.

"Stanley," she called out in steady, measured words, "— Come A-Bout. Come A-Bout. Do-you-hear-mee, Stanley? Come-A-Bout. You are A-Bout to hit Cap-Tan Ern-nee's boat."

Alice, in hopes they would carry through the falsetto howl of the wind, had given her words as rich and strong a baritone timbre as she was able to. To Sven, watching Alice stand and shout and bend at the same instant to hold down her skirt, it came out looking and sounding like a clowning woman doing a tasteless imitation of an operatic baritone calling hogs. Hot embers of Spanish moss cooled to look like burnt straw; he felt his erection grow as limp as a sprained ankle.

"You must shout louder, Alice," said Sven sadly. "I think he can't hear you out there."

Captain Hall filled his favorite china mug with the morning's fourth helping of good, strong, boiled coffee, mixed in two heaps of dark brown sugar spooned from the box, topped the mug with three or so ounces of milk poured from the carton, and comfortably sat himself on the top of his after deckhouse. He always had a good view from there.

Then, raising a thumb in the manner of a great but lazy artist with a meticulous eye for detail, he carefully monitored the rate of approach of the *Lu Pan*. He was used to the hazards of living anchored out in a crowded harbor, and it was obvious to him that Stanley, hidden behind the boat's sails, was not looking where he was going.

He was not so rattled by what he saw as to suppose he had been singled out for persecution that day. Christ, the sun hadn't yet come up that morning when he lay in his bunk dreaming of easy-going days back in Bora Bora. In his dream, the toothless smile of Lilly-Oppa-Langtree was the equal of the pleasure he felt as together they played the old Tahitian slap-stick dance, she used to call it. "Hey, dat feel pretty good, huh, Captain Ernie," she would say. She was enormously fat and Captain Ernie loved her dearly. "You poke-stick dance dis way and dat. Mama Oppa fix it good." He dreamt.

Then, WHANG. That's when the goddamn U.S. Customs Service patrol boat, snooping the bay for big-time contraband as always it did in the calm predawn hours, struck and severed Captain Ernie's stern anchorline.

What the two agents disguised as vacationing lumberjacks did that morning was in Captain Ernie's book about the dumbest thing that two landlubbers can do. Bumbling into his anchorline in the dark, that was one thing. But cutting it through with a knife after getting it tangled in the prop of their outboard motor—hell, for all they knew and cared they were cutting Captain Ernie adrift. If it weren't that he kept out a second anchor, run from the bow, they would have.

"Sorry about that," one of the undercover Feds told Captain Ernie. "We're just a couple of fishing fools from Oregon. For a minute there, we thought we had ourselves a salmon."

"Well, if you're really that stupid," Captain Ernie shouted back, "then you'll want to catch this right on the ends of your big, fat noses." Roused from sleep, standing stark naked on the afterdeck and peering down at them through the predawn murk, Captain Ernie let fly at the Feds' windshield with a 10-inch, cast-iron frying pan. Hell, everybody in the harbor knew these guys wearing the black-and-red checkered wool mack-inaws were Feds. They'd been running into people's boats in the dark for years.

The two feds—and this worried Captain Ernie—sped off in the darkness without saying a word. Christ, he'd busted their windshield but good. He would have gone to his bunk and summoned back Bora Bora and Mama Lilly-Oppa, but he knew the Feds had other ways of getting back at him—sic the IRS or the county tax people on him by way of a couple of quick phone calls. Other than that he'd rigged the boat here and there to look like a commercial salmon trawler so he could get a tax break on it and roll himself a nest egg that would be his back-to-Bora Bora money, there wasn't much anybody could pin on him. Here it was ten o'clock in the morning and no one had yet come snooping.

Well, be that what it was, he sure as hell wasn't going to let Stanley ruin his regular morning coffee break by ramming his yawl smack amidships. He drained the last of the coffee from his mug, went to the rail, raised his thumb and took measure as he had before. Then, waiting until the bow of the *Lu Pan* came to within just the right distance, which he figured to be about 10 yards, he took careful aim and threw the thick china mug as hard as he could.

It hit the right eye of the *Lu Pan* just above the eyebrow and shattered into fragments. "Bullseye," said Captain Ernie Hall.

Hours later, Stanley would describe the sound of it as "being like a temple gong struck at dawn deep in the interior of old-time China, or like a thump on a hollow log, as if ancient people squatted on a beach along the sea of time had warned the *Lu Pan* of danger ahead. Alice, you want to know what really happened?"

"What," Alice would say, "—why you swung the tiller around so fast? Stanley, you all but scared the pants off me. Boy, you swung the boat dead into the wind, just like that. It stopped like it had brakes on it, and next thing you're sitting broadside to Captain Ernie, like two ducks in a pond, and there he is reaching out to shake your hand. What the hell did he say, anyway? You must have scared the pants off him too."

"Actually, he was greatly impressed," said Stanley. "He says, 'That's one hell of a boat you got there, fella. The minute I saw those magic eyes staring at me, I figured anyone steering that boat don't need to see for himself, he's got the same kind of protection God gives drunks, kids, and fools, to save them from their own damned foolishness.'

"Alice, it's boat magic. We've got a magic boat. I don't know what it is. It's something you feel in your gut. You just know it's there. Everyone who has ever owned a boat feels that. They may not say it, but they get that certain feeling. Even Captain Ernie."

"Captain Ernie is into boat magic?" said Alice.

"Yeah," said Stanley. "He invites me aboard to have a drink. 'I'll fix you a rum punch,' he says. Then he takes me below and shows me this packing crate full of china coffee mugs he's got.

"'Some people paint eyes on their boats,' he says. 'Some call a priest and have the boat blessed. Me, I keep forty or fifty coffee mugs on hand at all times.'

"It took ten of them, he told me—but one night, off the coast of Singapore, the mugs saved him from being run down by a Greek freighter."

"Aw, he was pulling your leg," said Alice

"That's what I told him," said Stanley. "China mugs are china mugs. Pretty utilitarian stuff if you ask me. They got about the same magic in them as spoons and saucers. But he gave me such an odd look I knew better than to say another word.

"He pulls two mugs out of the box, fills them up with rum and grapefruit juice, about fifty-fifty of each. 'Here toast,' he says. 'You believe in your kind of magic, sailor, and I'll stick with the mugs. They're the best kind of boat collision insurance a man can buy.'"

Stanley spent the next several hours drinking mugs of rum and grapefruit juice with Captain Ernie and it was just as well that Stanley stayed out there the while. Back at the dock, back home, at the marina, events were taking a less than magical turn.

PART III

THE ULTIMATE GETAWAY BOAT

Chapter *11*

An Unforgettable Chicken Dinner, and How at Sea St. Elmo's Fire Lighted the Way Home

Potent Quotes

"The system, we have learned, gentlemen, cons the people in order to keep the system going. It only follows that the people must con the system in order to keep the people going. Boats, gentlemen—boats!"

> Smasden Kosinski, KMT,
> his Ninth Annual Address,
> Friends of Snow Planet
> Ski Touring & Small Boat
> Cruising Society

"Poets and clowns have always risen up against the oppression of creative thought by dogma. Their intimate wonder dissolves uncertainties, banishes fears, and undoes paralysis.

> Ivan Illich,
> *Tools of Conviviality*

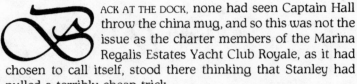ACK AT THE DOCK, none had seen Captain Hall throw the china mug, and so this was not the issue as the charter members of the Marina Regalis Estates Yacht Club Royale, as it had chosen to call itself, stood there thinking that Stanley had pulled a terribly cheap trick.

Sven, for one, and in his official capacity as Commodore-Elect of the newly formed club, was of the opinion that Stanley had been showing off, that he was trying to make the *Lu Pan* seem more than it was. Tilda Marbanks, who was there looking on, along with her husband Preston, had it in mind to write something nasty in the next issue of *The Porthole*, the Yacht Club Royale's monthly newsletter.

"What had started out as cute, if we can think of a highly unorthodox boat in this fashion," she would in fact write, "has turned the ugly duckling. Due to this and other unseemly events in matters of such harbor rules and regulations as affect the quality of life of others of us who live here too, the owners, we all know, have not been admitted to yacht club membership."

No sooner had news of this come percolating down the yacht harbor grapevine—before even the first issue of *The Porthole* had hit the docks—than Stanley and Alice were devastated by it. "It was sort of like getting notice from the insurance company that your car insurance has just been cancelled," said Alice. "In our case, we'd got rid of the car three years ago and didn't intend to buy another one ever. Our plan was to get away from all that. Living in this yacht harbor, we discovered, was somehow pushing us backwards in time—we were right back in the car and looking for the next off-ramp."*

---

*This is neither an idle nor misplaced allusion that Alice makes.

Sir Anton Ritter-LaRue, in a test conducted along heavily urbanized coastal areas in the U.S., has shown that automobiles and the car culture in general exert a much greater influence on yacht harbors than previously had been thought.

Using the Hobart Remote-Electrographic Method of determining to what extent cars shape minds, Sir Anton has been able to conclude that the more cars and the greater the size of the parking lot, the greater the likelihood that this is going to put a damper on the naturally congenial setting that is the yacht harbor.

"At worst and at best, the once quiet cove becomes a congested cul de sac, a busy-bee car park at the end of the road that leads to the sea.

"Thursday night," the news in *The Porthole* went on, "we plan to meet on Sven's 57-foot power cruiser for that wonderful slide show he's been promising of his 1956 trip across the bay to Martinez. Hint to Commodore-Elect Sven: did you find a bulb to fit the projector? Preston has promised (hint, hint, again) not to forget to put the Lemon Pepper in the clam dip—he's such a good chef if he puts his mind to it. . . ."

Preston Marbanks, in addition to preparing the official club clam dip (and remembering, if he would, to pick up fresh potato chips at the supermarket), was charged with running off the newsletter on the Xerox machine at his office downtown.

Preston was vice-president of a small company that manufactured cat food cans, and in anticipation of retiring soon on not too great an income, he had bought a used 45-foot motorsailer and talked Tilda into their living on it. Tilda had founded the newsletter, among other things, to give voice to strong feelings that the boating life had to be made civilized. Her preference had been to buy a townhouse in one of the adult retirement communities where the grounds were kept freshly mowed, the living room furniture perfectly arranged, the rugs held firmly to the floor by tacks and nails.

The trouble with living on a boat was that always it was riding up and down on the tide, which gave her the sensation of being in an elevator car that went the wrong way no matter which button she pushed. The wind blew and knocked things about. Every Sunday morning, when Preston ran the engine and charged batteries, picture frames crept askew.

Every day of the week, every hour of the day, were seagulls, a dirty dozen at a time, wheeling out of a clean blue sky to show themselves as ruinous to the furniture of the boating life as were ornery cats to rugs. One afternoon, while mopping up after them, she slipped on the wet deck. She caught herself by

---

"At night, while appearing to be just sitting there, each in its apportioned stall, cars in great numbers exert a psychic force. The harbormaster in his sleep dreams he is a traffic cop. Sleepers in the boats about the harbor toss and turn and dream of getting traffic tickets. The yacht harbor social fabric itself, after night after night of exposure to this, takes on a peculiar kinetic stress that is of the quality of the parked car sitting with the brake on in stasis, a tensed ghost in hobbles heard grinding its teeth the night long.

"To add to this apparitional setting by installing mercury vapor lamps that make everything a pink-grapefruit color, as always the harbor management does, borders on lunacy."

flinging the head of the mop into the ratlines and holding fast to the handle. But her spraycan of Lysol disinfectant went tumbling over the side and into the water.

Breeze and tide quickly carried the can beyond reach of first the mop and then a boat hook. "Help," she shouted. And then suddenly appeared a face in the water. It had whiskers like Felix the Cat, eyes like two black olives, a bald head as slick and smooth as volcanic glass. "Ark," it said, and took the can of Lysol in its mouth. "Thief," shouted Tilda Marbanks. "Thief!"

"Ark," it said again, and then seemed to smile as it vanished from the scene of the crime as quickly as it had appeared, leaving behind not a single clue as to where it might have gone. Tilda, for as long as she was able, kept her eyes on the expanding ring of ripples. But after a while those vanished too. She sensed an ineffable danger that day, a chill like that of the depth of the sea itself. Dark shapes rose and fell in the murky gloaming of this sea, and clearly were they up to no good.

"It did seem unlikely that a Black man, from the Fillmore district, most likely," she wrote in the next issue of *The Porthole*, "would be swimming in broad daylight in the harbor proper with rape and pillage in mind. One never knows these days. The incident did make me think to point out to the yacht harbor management that though they have promised to install locked gates to protect us from the land, there is nothing to prevent undesirable marauders from entering by way of the sea.

"Preston, the man of our boat, I must add, is equally alarmed. He has suggested the installation of a gate at the harbor mouth that is opened and closed by means of a call box directly linked to the harbor office. Persons coming and going will just have to stop and identify themselves."

Harbormaster and Vice President of Marina Regalis Estates Waterfront Properties and Condominium Developments Admiral-Carpenter Golfshoes Renfrow was having his problems at the harbor, too. "Gates? They want swinging gates at the harbor entrance?" he said to his wife one night as they lay in bed having sex. He was on top trying to get her legs open and she was trying to read a furniture ad in peace, in a small basement apartment on Chestnut Street where they sprouted avocado seeds in the kitchen window. "They're a bunch of goddamned turkeys down there," he told his wife.

"You're no great shakes yourself," she said. "I'm trying to read and you're getting cigarette ashes all over me."

Retired Chief Petty Officer, USN, Renfrow did not know what to make of civilians. He didn't know what motivated them, and since none of them wore their names on their clothes, printed with regulation stencils and white paint, he sometimes couldn't remember which one was which.

He had forgotten what the owners of Marina Regalis Estates looked like, too. Not since they had had their picture taken for the newspaper on the day of the groundbreaking ceremony had the Los Angeles–based six developers and six presidents ever again come north to see how things were going up there.

All he could recall of them was that they had arrived in a pink Cadillac limousine with a huge papier maché shovel tied to a luggage rack on top—and even the picture that appeared in the back pages of the local paper a week after the event showed only six pairs of pitch black sunglasses peering from behind the shovel's thick handle, looking like tree frogs perched on a log, as the shovel was theatrically levered into the pasty, red ooze that was to be the marina parking lot.

No sooner had the press picture been snapped than did the six pairs of sunglasses scurry back into the Cadillac and pull down the window shades. The door on the driver's side opened. A woman dressed in black got out, went to the Cadillac's trunk and opened it. From it, she removed a large cardboard box and what appeared to be a rolled-up map.

She went to Renfrow and asked could he read blueprints, and when he said he was no expert but could probably figure it out after a while, she gave him the copy of the architect's master plan and the box full of four-color sales brochures. "You're in charge, Renfrow," she said. "Don't fuck up."

"Yes, ma'm," said Renfrow. He felt an urge to salute the woman snappily. But on second thought, sensing that his business with her was not yet complete, he said, "If something goes wrong—if problems should get in the way, I mean to say, ma'm—how do I get in touch?"

The woman in black used a finger to lift one side of a gauzy black veil and make a narrow slit. A red eye, wet with tears and an oozy smudge of purple-green mascara, glowered at Renfrow.

"Send roses, you dolt," she said. "You don't know who I am, do you?"

"No, ma'm," he said crisply. "But if you give me the address, I'll be sure to send roses if the plumbing goes haywire. That's the first thing that happens when you're building a new marina, you know."

"Good," said the woman. "You follow instructions well. We can count on you to fully represent our interests here. Remember, Renfrow—keep your eyes on the Stars. Each snug in the sky, set like jewels. Think of the sky as a magnificent yacht harbor, Renfrow, its perfect docks *A* and *B* and *C* on through *Z* set in time forever. Big boats, little boats. Rudolph Valentino's old power cruiser. He loved that boat. Oh, Renfrow, I cry."

"Yes, ma'm," said Renfrow. "But I'll need to have the address."

"It is a mission, not a job we give you, Renfrow," said the woman. "Yours is to arrange the stars in rows, each a jewel in its perfect setting. Keep all in order here.

"Myrna Loy, Garbo, Zazu Pitts, the Marx Brothers, Harold Lloyd—Valentino's old power cruiser. Stanford University shall one day acquire that magnificent old relic and the bottom will be coming out of it. My astrologer is never wrong. Oh, Renfrow, I cry. Sing along with it, Renfrow. Salute the Stars.

"Marina Regalis Estates is to be Gateway to the Heavens. Don't forget that, Renfrow. Cast out the false, the flawed, all the two-bit stuff. All that floats does not necessarily glitter. Oh, I cry. Hand out brochures at every opportunity. There's bread and butter in this."

"I know my job, ma'm," said Renfrow. He thought it right now to deliver a snappy salute. He did. The woman in black got back into the pink Cadillac and drove it off, headed back south, to LA, with the six developers and six presidents of Marina Regalis Estates. That was the last he ever saw of any of them.

As plans for spiffy West Coast marinas and yacht harbors go, the Marina Regalis Estates was a dandy. The sales brochures were just as impressive. Authentic grass shacks and palm trees were to be imported whole from Tahiti, huge stone faces from Easter Island. The veranda of the Hotel Raffles in Singapore, an entire antique and still operative train from the mountain kingdom of Punjab. The Hawaiian King Kamehameha's (1758?–1819) old surfboard was to "adorn the Yacht Club's private bar and self-service grill," promised the sales brochure, "along with a section of the old Malibu fishing pier. Round and round the bar service area will go the Little Train from Punjab, making frequent stops so that passengers desiring to get *off* can and those desiring to get *on* can do that too.

"Our singing chef from Tonga will nightly be on hand to show yacht club members and their guests how to roast Coney Island Red Hots on a stick, but he will delight you most when suddenly he drops everything and does what he is most famous for. Before your eyes, using but two railroad spikes, the singing chef from Tonga, ratta-tat-tat, never ruining a block of 50-pound ice, in thirty seconds flat, carves perfect replicas every time of Bing Crosby and the Andrews Sisters. No other yacht club on the West Coast can make this claim."

Of all the stuff that had to do with the Salute to the Stars theme cooked up by the marina's developers, Renfrow liked best the part about Frankie Laine's coming up north once a month to do a Sunday evening community sing-along. And "Rawhide," thought Renfrow, was one helluva good song to do it with. Yes, Frankie Laine roaming the docks, tilts and nods of the head encouraging boat owners and their guests to sing-along as Frankie strummed the guitar and bellowed.

"Boat owners wearing western garb on these occasions," said the sales brochure, "will get special consideration in the determination of where their boats are to be placed about the harbor." Ah, that was Renfrow's job—to be certain that the most attractive boats in the marina—the clean, the white, the spic-and-span, the pretty and perfect—were placed like jewels, adorning the harbor's lacework of docks and fingerslips, the jewels' picture-perfect setting—this to conform to what the sales brochure promised those who would buy Marina Regalis

Estates waterfront condominiums. "Sunday evening, when the sun is setting in the western sky," said the sales brochure, "is the perfect time to look out the living room window, each with Thermopane double-sealed glass shutting out the Bay's frequent damp and cold." And there would it be seen, a perfection for the eye. The little boats, the docks and fingerslips.

The great thing about having the turkeys sing along to "Rawhide" and wear the western garb, thought Renfrow, was that if they didn't sing and didn't wear the stuff—well, that made his job a lot easier. He could tell at a glance which were the good turkeys and which were the bad—the potential troublemakers, the fuck-ups, the wimps, the refusers, the boat-rockers. No ten-gallon Stetson, no Tony Lama boots—these would be the people to keep an eye on. He'd know to bear down on these like a wet sponge on true grit.

"When Frankie Laine comes, would you take me to see him?" said Renfrow's wife one night. They were downtown at a discount mart looking over Reclino-Chairs that had been marked down 20 percent in an ad that had appeared in the Sunday paper.

Renfrow turned pale. "The hell with the Reclino-Chair," he said bitterly. "We're going home."

"You don't like the color?" said his wife.

Renfrow's dentures clacked, his mind ground in turmoil. He felt ground down and put-upon. The woman in black and the six developers and six presidents must have been on dope when they dreamed up Marina Regalis Estates, he reasoned.

There were no palms and thatched shacks from Tahiti, the stone faces from Easter Island had not arrived as promised, nor had the Samoan dance group, the hot tubs, the singing ice carver from Tonga, the Little Train from Punjab. Frankie Laine hadn't so much as shown up to whistle "Dixie."

"The trouble with those assholes and their big ideas," he blurted out at last, "is that they don't have any money and don't know a goddamned thing about building a marina. They can't even keep the place stocked in toilet paper."

"It's that bad?" said his wife. "You can't take a moment to decide which chair you want? Green or brown, sweetie, that's all they've got."

"Brown," sputtered Renfrow. He began throwing punches in the air. His sniffs were snorts, his inhales and exhales pops and wheezes.

To be sure, down at the marina, docks were sinking on the spot as a result of cheap and flawed construction, the waterfront condos weren't getting finished because the contractor was in court suing to get paid, the last storm from the south had overcome the shoddy breakwater and badly banged up two yachts, the showers had no hot water, half the toilets were out of order.

"It sort of makes you wonder what we're doing here," wrote Alice in her boating diary, in the section she had entitled, *Yacht Harbors and Marinas and Other Places to Visit that You Wouldn't Want to Live in if You Had Any Choice in the Matter.* "But You Got to Park the Boat Somewhere. It's a Goddamned Problem."

Chapter *12*

A Car-Park Comes to Valhalla, but the Vikings Have Boats and Won't Pay

Potent Quote

"I have poems; I can read. Tomorrow I shall hoist my sail, with fallen maple leaves behind me . . ."

—Li Po,
*Thoughts of Old Time From A
Night-Mooring Under Mount
Niu-Chu*

I N THE YEAR 906, Sir Anton Ritter-LaRue believes it was, this man who called himself Sven The Viking was sailing down the coast of Cornwall, along the southwest tip of the British Isles. Sven, for one, enjoyed going south for the winter, and he decided to stop at this place.

"Hello," he shouted out to the harbormaster upon approaching the guest dock, Sir Anton tells us in his book of odd sea tales. "This is a nice little marina you have here. How much you charge me to tie up the boats for the night?"

Sven thought he had been quoted an exorbitant price, but it was argued back that this marina was one of the few about that had fresh water conveniently located. Sven asked about good restaurants, but was frankly told there wasn't anything to be found close by. However, the marina did maintain one of the finest chicken franchises in the region—good, fresh Cornish roasting hens, made available on an attractively priced "you-catch, you-pluck" basis.

Sven was feeling considerably more expansive than usual that fall evening. His flotilla was of three swift long boats and a fourth, a slower cargo vessel, each heavily laden with a lot of used furniture and sundry household items obtained during a quick stop along the way.

"Included in this mess of stolen pottage," Sir Anton tells us, "were the wives and daughters of half a dozen or so Celtic potato farmers.

"In a runic inscription later found—and wherever they went the Vikings were always leaving behind these little stone billboards of theirs—Sven says it was the women's idea to quit the farm and take up the boating life. 'We get mud up to our knees just going up to the place,' inscribed Sven with a chisel. 'But these women, they have to live in this stuff. One tells me she does all the work with the hoe. The husband sits drunk by the fire all day.

"'Come to sea in a sleek boat,' I tell her. 'Wash the mud off in good, clean seawater. Listen to the whales sing. Always the sea is fresh and blows the stink of the land away. You see what I mean when you try it. Let geezers who think they own you poke sticks in the mud and grow the potatoes and see how they like it for a change.

"'The women say I make a good idea. They pull up their skirts and run to the boats before we do. I figure, now we go find a cozy little marina and have a good time. We start a new life together, Sven and his boats and men and these women with the blue eyes and freckles and the lovely white teeth.'"

Well, there is nothing like a good picnic to get a propitious event off on the right foot. No sooner had they properly checked in at the marina office and paid the required moorage fees than did Sven and his bunch purchase several hundred plump hens from the local concessionaire and as many crocks of the unusually fine Cornwall birch-honey mead as they could get their hands on.

Indeed, it wasn't long before chicken feathers fell like snow flakes as twenty or thirty of Sven's men sat high in the rigging of their ships wringing necks and plucking hens. They threw the carcasses down to the waiting hands of men stationed fire brigade-fashion the entire length of the guest dock.

While doing the sort of stomp-kick, hetcha-hetcha-hetcha, stiff-legged hop-dance that always accompanies the Viking chicken-plucking song, the men on the dock flung the chickens one to the other, the last man hurling his to a bear skin stretched taut in the hands of a circle of ships' cooks. The cooks sang the Viking chicken-cooking song and did the hetcha-hetcha, stomp-kick, hop-dance that always accompanies that song too.

When the bear skin was so full-up it was almost more than they could carry (the men on the dock every so often in jest would heave a ship's ballast stone or two into the blanket), the cooks would dance it over to the largest of the bonfires built hours before in the lovely meadow that was the marina's public picnic area and park. The cooks in perfect unison—one, two, three, all together now—blanket-tossed the plucked birds whole into the fire, where they were stirred with long sticks by several young apprentices working under the strict supervision of Sven's personal chef, who was also the fleet navigator-shaman, physician-dentist, barber-chemist, and what have you.

Several of the Celtic women helped the chef with the seasoning, which they did by dancing naked about the fire and rubbing themselves all over with bay leaves as the chicken sizzled and cooked. Every so often, as the recipe required, the chef threw in the fire a bucketful of the one condiment that all were just crazy about, a concoction of his that he called Thor's Best and which mostly consisted of finely ground sea salt and potassium nitrate, in addition to a small amount of a secret ingredient that he would reveal to no one, not even Sven. Azure blue flames burst forth with each heave of the bucket. A kind of thunder clapped, mushroom clouds of thick, white smoke spiraled skyward.

When seen to have cooked to just the right do, which was a difficult-to-achieve combination of finger-licking good and burnt to a crisp, with especially the skin as black and crunchy as any good charcoal briquet, a chicken was pulled out of the fire at the point of a spear and then catapulted pell-mell into the meadow, where a Viking raider was sure to catch it on the fly and score himself a perfect chicken dinner.

While waiting for their dinner to arrive, others in the meadow partook of such leisure time activities as wrestling matches and sword fighting contests. Games of tug-of-war and blindman's buff were also popular. Arms and legs were lost, eyes punched out, referees and umpires pushed into fires.

Well, the party was just getting underway in this fasion when one of the apprentices working the spear got it in mind to throw a cooked chicken farther than anyone there could run to catch it, and it flew a good distance indeed, beyond his wildest expectations, even. It landed in the lap of the snoozing harbormaster. Right through his harbor office window and smack into his lap fell the scorched, blazing hot, charcoal black remains of a once-great little Cornish roasting hen.

The harbormaster and his board of directors did not welcome the kind of disorderly conduct seen going on down at the public picnic area and in the vicinity of the guest dock. Sign boards, with strict regulations against just this sort of thing printed as plain as day, had been posted in all the appropriate areas.

Marina regulations specifically required, among other things, that "Swords and shields must be neatly stacked away from public walking areas. Campfires and cookouts are permitted only with prior permission, for which potential participants are required to give several days' notice due to the overwhelming popularity of the new barbecue facilities now located in the clubhouse. Chickens are to be plucked in the area provided and feathers deposited in refuse baskets made available at the harbor office for a nominal fee."

That Sven and his band of ruffians had violated the harbor and environs code of public conduct, that was one thing, the harbormaster told Sven after running down to the picnic area to complain. But for his men to have torn down and burned the signs without their first having made the effort to read the rules and regulations clearly printed on them—that took the cake!

"What are you talking about?" said Sven. "Already you charge me too much to tie up the boats for the night—and now you tell me there are rules and regulations?

"Any good marina I know of doesn't treat its public this way. You don't even provide a decent stick of dry wood to start the bonfires with. Sure we use your stinking signs."

"You, sir, and those unruly women you bring," said the harbormaster, "have been observed cavorting about an illegal campfire, one set on city property, I must add. This is a violation of city ordinances on at least two counts I can think of. If I must call a constable, my good man, you may consider you and your group eligible for some very stiff fines indeed.

"If you will take my advice, and if I may say this without offending your barbarian pride, here are your horned hats, sir. Take them and go without delay."

"What is this I hear—are you crazy?" said Sven. "You tell us fellows to pack up and go before even we have a chance to eat our chickens in peace?"

"If I were to make it any plainer than I already have," said the harbormaster, "you might think me nasty."

"Oh, so now you want to be nasty," said Sven. "Well, now I must tell you something. You insult us without first looking to see what kind of people you are talking to. Look over there— what do you think he is doing?"

"It's only too obvious what the gentleman is doing," said the harbormaster. "He's disgustingly drunk and urinating on the roof of our clubhouse."

"No, no," said Sven. "Some cinders started a fire up there. He is getting old. He is showing a sense of civic responsibility. But that is not the man I mean. It is the one by the fire holding the chicken."

"Chicken halves, you mean to say," said the harbormaster. "Good Lord, he's been cleaved in two down the middle with a sharp instrument and he's still standing with dinner in hand. Was it something he said? An ingracious remark to the gentleman over there with the battle axe?

"Having hacked up his friend, was it, I see now he's hacking up the hedgerow put there by the improvement club only last spring."

"No, no," said Sven. "You don't get the point. He is working off steam. The one with the chicken said a very nasty thing to him. Now, what you tell me—that is my point. You don't tell a Viking to pack up and go when he's having some good, clean fun, and expect him to kiss your feet."

Sven, who was never without his battle horn hanging about his neck, raised and blew it. Four strong blasts followed by a short pause, and then a long, hard final blast of a much lower pitch. It was the coded twang at the end that informed Sven's men that they were being kicked out of yet another badly run marina and had been roundly insulted to boot: level the lousy place.

Only because he ran off to get the town constable the moment the mayhem started was the harbormaster spared his being roasted over a fire and then tied to a post set at well below the high-tide mark, but one more of Viking customs that sorely tried his patience.

When the harbormaster did get back to the marina (having had to ride behind the constable on the back of an aged mare), there was scarcely a Viking in sight—only a very old fellow, in fact, with a long beard, who had passed out in a treetop early on during the party. From what the constable was able to deduce from the scene, other Vikings, as they went about their work of thoroughly dismantling the marina, had chopped down the tree without knowing the old one was up there. He tumbled down when the tree fell and had inadvertently been left on the spot, in a heap of twigs and broken branches. The constable instantly put him under arrest.

Nowhere about were more Vikings to be seen. Boats, baggage, and plunder, Sven and his bunch were gone, and it was obvious they'd left in a huff. The guest dock, it was observed, had been heaped with shrubs, entire sections of decorative hedges and partitioning fences, park benches, trees torn out by the roots, a sizeable assortment of civic commemorative statues—all of it burning with a roar as the dock, set adrift and pushed along by a changing tide, made for the open sea.

What baffled the constable was trying to figure out how in the world the Vikings had managed to drag the harbormaster's log office down to the water's edge and set that adrift, too, upside down, so that it bobbed about in the harbor like an odd square boat with eccentrically placed doors and windows.

In his book, Sir Anton explains that "this feature of retrospective Viking presence on dry land, an element he was never altogether at home with, is not in the cultural perspective of his mind-set an odd one. It was a symbolic gesture, a statement of his great preference for boats over houses generally. To him, a house was an upside-down boat, as was clearly indicated in the structural elements of his houses of worship, with their beams and rafters perfectly replicating the keelsons and ribs of his ships.

"In a bad mood, feeling trapped and put-upon by the land and its ways, he was able to put his world right again by turning houses upside down and pushing them back into the sea, where they belonged."

In any event, when all had been said and done at Cornwall, the municipal marina was in such a sad state of disrepair, as indeed the harbormaster sized it up for benefit of the board of directors, that it was going to take until 1927 to raise funds enough to put it fully back together and to plant more and better signs stating the local rules and regulations.

To be sure, when 1927 did come round, the new signs were fashioned of fireproof sheet metal riveted to good, stout steel poles anchored in the ground with deeply set cement cannisters. To this day, one of the largest of these signs stands at the seaward end of the New Guest Dock, as still the locals call it. "This is a Nice Little Marina," it says. "Vikings and Other Similarly-Minded Persons Applying for Moorage Space Must Pay in Advance and Leave a Sizeable Deposit."

One of the more interesting features of the marina, certainly, is the Old Cornwall Municipal Port Authority Office. This is seen to be floating still, just as upside down as it was in the year 906, rising and falling with the tide. Stout anchor and chain hold it fast to the original rock upon which it came to stop not long after the Vikings had set it adrift. A tour-boat concession for a small fee offers excursions to it several times daily.

"Captain Nemo," writes Sir Anton, "was of course no more a Viking than the Vikings were yachtsmen, but he had his run-ins with yacht harbors and marinas, too." Specifically which marinas and yacht harbors, Sir Anton doesn't say, nor is there much in the way of detail. Sir Anton gets his information from private notes of Jules Verne's, and even then, when we expect more, we learn only that "Nemo got himself kicked out of a snooty yacht club in colonial India as the result of an untoward incident in the club bar. A public thrashing had been scheduled by member naval officers, but Nemo put to sea in the submarine *Nautilus* and never came back."

In any event, and as Sir Anton goes on about it, "Captain Nemo, completely self-sufficient in an undersea empire of his own contrivance, has this to say: 'I have done with society entirely, for reasons which I alone have the right of appreciating. I do not therefore obey its laws.'*

"In this philosophical gesture, Captain Nemo epitomizes in sanguine fact what the Vikings could only imagine and long

---

*Walter James Miller, in his annotated edition of Twenty Thousand Leagues Under the Sea, also makes an observation about this business. ". . . The captain clearly states the position of the Higher Conscience, the Great Refusal, in effect summarizing the message of H. D. Thoreau's Civil Disobedience (1849) and foreshadowing the worldwide 'dropout' movement of the 1960s and 1970s."

for, as they were getting themselves kicked out of marinas and yacht harbors wherever they went. It is only Captain Nemo who is able to put to sea and remain there to enjoy the one and great open expanse that is the freedom of the sea itself. Out of sight, out of mind. Civilization and its nonsense becomes but a stilled noise long gone over the horizon.

"In this vast littoral zone of the aquatic existence, the land ends, the sea begins. This zone of entry and interface is, as the Vikings discovered long before us, no more Valhalla than is a pay-by-the-month parking stall in midtown Manhattan."

Chapter *13*

The Captain's Hard-Times Holiday on the Way Back to Bora Bora, and a Perfect Bowl of Hot Burgoo

Potent Quotes

*"Enjoy yourself, relax
stop setting snares . . .
Be simple and plain
and follow where that leads you.
Go find yourself a place to flop
and flop there."*

Kuan Han-ch'ing
a winter tune

*"Tereza paused and said softly, 'The best thing to do would
be to move away.'
'I agree,' said Tomas, 'but there's nowhere to go.'"*

Milan Kundera
The Unbearable Lightness of Being

APTAIN ERNIE HALL, FOR one, is a great believer in anchoring out and avoiding marinas altogether. If you do it right, there's self-sufficiency and independence in this, he says—a lot of personal satisfaction. To make this work, you need at least two good anchors and lots of stout line and lengths of chain, plenty of space to let the boat swing freely with the tide and not bang into other boats that are anchored out and swinging too, and, not least of all, a seaworthy dinghy and two good oars to row it with. You use the dinghy as you would a car, say, to get back and forth to market, to fetch fresh water and supplies, visit friends, and, on a nice day, maybe take a "ride," get some fresh air, and what have you. *Row, row, row your boat,* if not always gently. Splish-splash the oars, up and down the seaway. There is no road tax, traffic cops and service station attendants don't know you even exist, a driver's license is not required. In a way, you become invisible.

Sometimes when anchored out you wake up to find the dinghy seats sopping wet with dew and sea-slop and the bilge filled to the brim, and so you have to bail and dry the thing out before you can row ashore to maybe a hot breakfast of sausage and eggs on some grunty, gray morning when you just don't feel like cooking. Rags and sponges, rubber boots—you need these too when you're anchored out and using the dinghy to get there and back again. Car seats never get wetted in this fashion, but then cars don't have oars, they don't float, they won't go anywhere when they run out of gas.

Anchoring out has its hazards, most of which, as Captain Hall is quick to point out, are not the physical ones that come of being exposed to the vagaries of wind and tide and dragging anchors ("Those I can relish and can damned well contend with," he says, for instance), but the societal ones originating on land—getting bugged and checked upon as more and more these days the forces and entities that regulate the flat, dry regions of the planet want to regulate the waters too, and it is bad bread they cast upon them, he thinks.

It had gone on to become a year now, and, for him, a very long year, since Captain Hall sailed into San Francisco Bay after a long haul down the coast from southeastern Alaska, always a favorite stop of his. He had a friend in Juneau, a contractor who built docks up and down the coast up there and lived on an old World War II PT boat. They would go crabbing in the PT boat on Auk Bay, catch a sackful, boil them up, on the spot and with the anchor out, over an antique cast-iron stove fired up with Alaska coal gathered, by the chunk, from a beach. Captain Hall was fond of fresh-cooked crab and long talks over drinks while eating the crab. But there were long, dark winter nights of constant, chilling drizzle up there, and so, as always, he headed south come November.

San Francisco Bay, that was a favorite stop too, and he liked to anchor off "the little village of Sausalito," as he referred to this once great little backwater from highly personalized memory of long, long ago. In those days, at night, when the fog came in and the fog horns blew, when deserted streets were slick and smelled of seaweed, you felt a great sense of removal and isolation. In those days, the place was a village, a half-forgotten sea town in a state of near ruin like that of the old ferry run up on the mudflats. It was Funkville, Anything-Goes-Ville. You could pull a dory up on the beach, put a tent over it, call it home. You wouldn't be noticed.

Now, when weekend traffic jammed narrow streets with rivers of tourists, as developers and their minions of officialdom tidied and prettied the place and put it up for sale to the chic and the affluent—well, it was still a great place if you closed one eye and remembered it from way back when. Quaint villages along the bay's backwaters, when set too close to urban areas, before long become towns, towns cities. And if you hung around too long, you'd have to close both eyes to make it work. No, it was just another stop and an old haunt. Captain Hall hadn't planned to stay any longer than it would take, by hook or crook, to gather up a fistful of tens, twenties, fifties—seed money, moving-on money, to add to the small but steady retirement checks granted a skipper of sea tugs and formerly in the service of a Taiwan ship salvage company.

He never told anyone, actually, how much those checks were, or, for that matter, what was the name of the company he'd worked for over twenty years in the Orient. For reasons he wouldn't reveal, you could never get from him a straight answer about this. "Hell, I'm just an old pirate," he'd say, "sort of in retirement these days, like the rest of them. Never paid much anyway, and the retirement's even worse. Make more money now buying and selling junk here and there." Old screen doors, for instance. Like Captain Nemo, you would come to realize, Captain Hall played it close to the vest and kept an air of mystery about himself. "You've got to survive"—that was all he ever said about this.

In any event and whatever was to be the denouement of this sea tale (and just shortly before Alice and Stanley and the *Lu Pan* were to get kicked out of Marina Regalis Estates [they were, really?]), Captain Hall, after throwing the frying pan through the undercover Fed's prowl boat—well, he was soon and early one morning paid a visit by a Coast Guard bay patrol boat. The officer in charge had charged out from shore to inspect Captain Hall's fire extinguishers. Were they regulation ones? Were they pumped up, Sir, to full pressure?

No sooner did he satisfy that sudden, urgent concern of land-based officialdom's than was he visited by a tax investigator, sent by the county, who demanded, through a smile as broad as the river Rio Grande on the first warm day of spring, to see the receipts Captain Hall had for all the crabs, salmon, flounder, bullheads, and catfish he claimed to have sold to a local fish and chowder house.

Could Captain Hall, it was asked point-blank, prove that he had not cheated the county out of taxes regularly levied against pleasure boats by claiming the special exemption granted bona fide commercial fishermen? Privately, Captain Hall steamed at the idea that the county defined his as a pleasure boat on the convenient notion that his and any boat not commercially employed was the toy of a rich man. Only a Mexican bandit or, worse, land people sitting in suit pants and swivel chairs would dream up such a scheme, he was righteously convinced, and have the gall to make it law so that the law, when push came to shove, could do what no bandit could, which was put you in jail for refusing to hand over the money in a stick-up. The pleasure of *his* boat, fumed Captain Ernie, was in its being house and home, mobile as a lark on the wind, cheap living if you knew how—and goddamned if he wanted tax people reaching out from the shore to mess up his scheme.

Outwardly, Captain Hall had acted on the precept, borrowed, so to speak, from a boating friend (Smasden Kosinski, about whom we shall hear more soon), that any system that cons the people should by the people be conned right back. The trawling poles Captain Hall had set up in the rigging certainly looked authentic enough from a distance, and the tax investigator was of a mind to compliment Captain Hall on this. He'd seen far worse attempts of this kind, he said. But the fact was, that if you did get up close, as the tax man had, it was easy to figure out that Captain Hall had trimmed branches from a stand of Eucalyptus growing along the railroad tracks down the shore a way from where Captain Hall was anchored. No lines, no hooks or spinners to be seen or found anywhere on the boat. The tax man smiled at Captain Hall like a Mexican bandit with a law degree from Harvard, shook his hand heartily, and said, "This is a fraud. We gotcha."

Old pirates never die, and certainly not as the result of a minor setback caused them by a Mexican bandit *cum laude* with a smile like plate glass that you couldn't shatter with a sledge hammer dipped in wild pig shit: they smile back ("Have a nice day, muchacho"), drop everything, and get the hell out of town on the first good tide. In Captain Hall's case, Hawaii called, and it called that instant. *Hey, Cap'n Ernie,* it said. *You get your ass over here fast.* And that's what Captain Ernie did. But Hawaii was to be just a stop along the line, too—a 24-hour Denny's on the night road to Byzantium, a pit stop along the Möbius strip of red sails hot in pursuit of fireball sunsets, a pothole in the speed lane.

Yes, no. Hawaii was for Captain Hall much too civilized, a new freeway in the wilderness. The Hawaiians were into fast Japanese cars and gold-plate Italian trinkets, rings, bracelets, toothpicks, as seen on TV. Like most of Western civilization and its distant possessions, the islands were too far gone on the way to becoming just another traffic jam, a crowded parking lot, a rush on a fashion shopping mall. No, Hawaii was not his Gucci bag.

And so from there, after taking on a rag-tag cargo of fascinating junk (*more* old screen doors, some stout if warped lengths of bamboo pole, bundles of old cedar shingles, a carton of old Japanese paper fans, several coils of manila rope of various diameters, a bunch of cast-iron pots and pans, all rusty but nothing a couple of Brillo pads couldn't take care of, and then this and that and so on and an old wood nail barrel full of the brass "corners" you use to take the wobble out of old table and chair legs), Captain Hall sailed on down to the Marshall Islands, to the capital atoll of Majuro, where he planned to sell all this junk of his. The indigenous folk of Micronesia, he knew, needed stuff like this to patch and fix their shack houses along the beach.

He didn't make much on this because he charged next to nothing, likely as not making a trade, a barter. A case of USDA canned pork, for instance, which the government had sent down there in its islands welfare program, and which the islanders couldn't stand and often as not fed to such live pigs as they had on hand, for say, three screen doors and maybe a cast-iron Dutch oven and a small egg pan.

A lot of the Marshall Islanders didn't have glass in the windows of their houses, nor doors in their front doorways, and so Captain Hall's old screen doors were here put to good use in either instance. Whole doors would be used to put front doors where before there were none. Sections of screens pulled from doors were tacked over windows to keep the flies out and to let the ocean breezes blow through the house, as glass would not allow and which is why the islanders—the smart, old-time ones anyway, the ones Captain Hall most liked—didn't much like glass, anyway.

In the Marshalls, where nowhere was there a chunk of the native land that stood more than the height of a man above sea level, Captain Hall felt closer to home—but not yet *there*, by any means. Again was this but a stopping place, a transition zone, as he saw it, a place to sweat in the oceanic equatorial heat—steam heat, as if the whole of the outdoors here were a Finnish sauna set to high and with the boiler about to blow—and to immerse oneself in an ocean that so overwhelmingly colored the quality of existence in this place of atolls awash in the depths of the Pacific. A place to get the foul stink of the land blow'd off a man, he put it, along the way to getting where really he was going.

Well, to get back to our point of concern here, which is that there are more ways than one to skip out on the system (having the right boat, anchors and line, and so on), certainly would it seem that Captain Hall has got it together in a way to be envied. When times get tough, the system gets out of hand, he hauls anchor, hoists sails, and goes. With him he has (and the boat must be seen to be included in the *with-him* part of it) most everything he needs to (1) just get up and go when he wants and (2) just keep on going if he wants. *Mobilus in Mobili. Sailing for the Sun. East, West, all around.* All birds of a feather.

So, in this book, this is the last we hear of Captain Ernie Hall. We leave him there in the Marshalls, in that steamy transition zone (he cooks, he coos, he cranks, he loves it) of his getting to where he's going next. That would be, we know, Bora Bora, and there, in those languid mini-hectares of emerald green and cobalt blue, Lilly Oppa-Langtree, after customs, will be first to come calling.

Ah, yes. There'll be a Tahitian stick dance in the cabin of the old boat that night, a hot time in the old tub that Captain Ernie Hall is pleased to call home. It floats, it sails, and, we must add in deference to future time, it *got* there. Aloha, *bonne nuit, bon appétit*, have a nice day, Captain Ernie. Until next time, then.

Alice and Stanley and the *Lu Pan* got themselves kicked out of Marina Regalis Estates, huh? Well, we're not terribly surprised about that. What happened was this, more or less:

Shortly after the *Lu Pan*'s trial run, in which it was established to the satisfaction of both that they had themselves a good seaboat, an honest-to-God voyager, Alice and Stanley had a dockside celebration, for which they cooked a couple of fat chickens on the old hibachi. They had a few drinks (some inexpensive but good cold duck drunk warm for lack of a refrigerator), made love under the down quilt covering the double-bunk in the *Lu Pan*'s forepeak, went to sleep soon after.* When they awoke the next morning, they first thing noticed that the hibachi left sitting on the dock the night was gone. Along with it had been taken a remaining half chicken, a would-be leftover that Alice had wrapped in aluminum foil and left sitting on the hibachi's blackened stainless steel grill.

What they found in the hibachi's and the chicken half's stead was a note—or a memorandum with a note written on it actually, and which at first glance didn't make a lot of sense.

"Persons not paying fee/fines for confiscated personal items within the 30-day period required," it said, "will have such fee/fine added on to the monthly moorage fee as prescribed by harbor rule and regulation." Commander Fee/Fine Fo Fum Two-Shoes had spent hours sitting in his harbormaster's office nights, tirelessly making erasures and breaking pencil points, to get the memorandum's wording just right. "Chains will be applied to boats of owners," this mopey mandate went on, "not paying such fee/fine in total amount at regular moorage fee due/date. Remember: a fee/fine paid on time is one less mark against your poor standing at Marina Regalis Estates."

The handcrafted and personalized note at the left upper edge

---

*Boating how-to fans will wonder about this: Why an apparently old-fashioned, down-filled quilt and not the new "Zip 2 Together" style of marine sleeping bag, one particular model of which features an attractive "Port" and "Starboard" pairing, each denoted by the appropriate color, red or green?

Well, for one thing, Alice and Stanley were on a tight budget, and so having to be tight and at the same time wanting to be snug and cozy, they went the old-fashioned quilt route (made it herself, Alice did, as we know), but with a modern, high tech twist: Alice had lined the quilt's underside with an acrylic flannel sheet. The advantage here is in the way acrylic flannel fights boat damp (no more clammy feet or, for that matter, clammy bare bottoms clinging to damp sheets that impede all movement and progress and what), keeps you warm and cuddled, as was the happy situation as Alice and Stanley freely squirmed and turned and made love under their quilt. Thick billows of Sausalito fog, as inimical to cotton or silk or nylon as spilled glue is to floors, enveloped the boat that night, seeped in through the tiniest cracks and crevices, but little did they care. Slick and quick under an acrylic flannel sheet (one beneath them too), high tech down under where every movement counts. Such clamminess as occurred was contained in all the right places, they stuck to it, and thanks to this new, all-absorbing sheeting, they in the end stuck to nothing save one another, snug as bugs in acrylic fur coats.

of the photocopied memorandum said, "Rules are rules. You left your hibachi sitting out on the dock all night. Fee/fine is $5. It's locked up in my office." Worse, and which made Stanley and Alice madder than hell, was that Cmdr. Marsh Marshall Flit-Fuss had chained the *Lu Pan* to the dock. He did this on the thought/hope that Alice and Stanley either couldn't/wouldn't pay the fee/fine. Alice and Stanley had a mind's eye picture (which wasn't far from right) of his having been stealthy in the night, quiet as a mouse, careful not to rattle the 20-foot length of steel chain, as he looped it about the *Lu Pan*'s mast and then, click/snap, used a stout lock to secure the chain's ends to a ringbolt fixed to the dock with tamperproof bolts. Did he then tiptoe off, in the thick of the Sausalito fog, on little cat/mouse feet, the hibachi and its chicken half cradled in the crook of an arm? Alice and Stanley thought it likely that he had.

Well, now, what to do about that/this, they wondered: pay the fee/fine and get back the hibachi and the chicken, and then Hildago Hilding Fast Fingers would unchain the boat, all would be restored to happy normalcy at Marina Regalis Estates?

"Not on your life," said Alice to Stanley. "It isn't the five bucks to get back the hibachi. It's the principle of the thing."

"You're goddamn right," said Stanley to Alice. "The only way to deal with impossible tyrants is to do the impossible right back at them."

"Which is?" said Alice.

"First off," said Stanley, "we cut the chain for a fast getaway. Commander Fleet-Foot will sic the cops on us no sooner than we kick in his door, grab the hibachi, and tell him to shove his fee/fine up his ass. We'll have to make a run for it."

"It's a perfect plan," said Alice. "But like any perfect plan, there's just one problem. The links of the chain holding the boat to the dock are half an inch thick and from what I can tell, made of steel imported from the planet Krypton. A fresh hacksaw blade won't put a scratch in it. I tried."

Stanley thought a moment. Captain Ernie, before *he* skipped town, had mentioned the name of a man capable of performing near-miracles, a dear friend of his who lived on a boat somewhere in the vicinity and owned a pair of the kind of bolt cutters that cops and crooks use to snip chains and locks as quick as the wink of a cockroach eyeing a cube of butter in its paper wrapper.

If ever he and Alice got into a pinch and it had anything to do with boats, boating, and the boating life, Stanley recalled Captain Ernie's having told him, go look up Smasden Kosinski. "The sonofabitch is Superman. Tell him Captain Ernie sent you." Aha, thought Stanley—that's it in a nutshell. And how right he was in his choice of semantics.

Chapter 14

A Sort of Jules Verne Mininovel, in Which Smasden Kosinski Gets the Best of Captain Nemo, and How the Bank Tried to Repossess the Nautilus

Potent Quote

"If his destiny be strange, it is also sublime."

Jules Verne, at book's end,
Twenty Thousand Leagues Under the Sea

BEFORE HE "GOT INTO boats," if we are to properly quote his writings on the subject, Smasden Kosinski was public relations director of the L. Gordon Strong Neckties Co., Ltd., with manufacturing plants in Taiwan and Cairo.

Kosinski, however, worked out of the San Francisco distributorship on Howard Street, "where the boss kept the box of silly neckties I used to have to show around to potential customers—and *they* weren't any great shakes, either. A traveling display case, this box was. It squeaked when you opened it, ha, ha, ha. I gave this crappy necktie business the old heave-ho—and I mean *all* of it. Get a boat and go for it, I told myself. It was Captain Nemo himself who put me up to the idea. 'Get thee to the bosom of the sea,' he says."

Alice had heard that actor Sterling Hayden, between movies and living on a Victorian-style houseboat down the way, had recently in the night caught Kosinski snapping pictures of him through the kitchen skylight. The local aquatic grapevine for days buzzed hot purple with news of this. Tilda Marbanks, as a matter of fact, ran a short item in *The Porthole*.

Hayden, it appeared, had not bought Kosinski's story that he had been hired by a boating how-to magazine "to get a great picture of Hayden preparing his famous Volga Boatman Beef Pattie." Actually, Hayden was at the time heating a pot of leftover bean soup. It had been long after midnight when he'd heard Kosinski crawling around on the roof. Tilda Marbanks called Hayden a day or two later and asked Hayden would he give her the Volga Boatman Beef Pattie recipe, she wanted to include this in her article. Hayden told her he had never heard of the "goddamned thing."

Hearing this, Tilda Marbanks got it in her head that Kosinski was a government man—"a creep spy for the Securities Exchange Commission. Big Brother is peering into our portholes nights.

"You can't fool us, Mr. *K*," she went on in her newsletter article, "—ask anyone what goes with *K*remlin that goes with

Inski-Pinski and has Russian boiled egg all over its face." What the hell this had to do with the Volga Boatman Beef Pattie incident was anyone's guess, and those who read the article and were able to make sense of it assumed that Tilda Marbanks had taken advantage of the incident to get off a cheap shot at the SEC. It was well known that Preston Marbanks was selling stocks out of his boat in some scheme to build a yacht clubhouse and then lease it out to the Marina Regalis Estates people. A stock purchaser had filed a complaint, and now the SEC was asking Preston questions.

If indeed there was any solid basis (something you could sink your teeth into) to the notion that Kosinski was in the business of ferreting secrets from out of the boating community—a reportedly good 60 percent of grapevine subscribers were saying he was—it was that Kosinski was in fact often seen prowling the local harbors and waterways in a battered old fishing dory, writing notes on scraps of paper and then stuffing these in his boat. Actually, Kosinski was writing a book—a rather odd boating journal.

What he had told his old friend Captain Ernie (Captain Ernie had then passed this story on to Stanley, Stanley to a captivated Alice) was that Captain Nemo ("*The* Captain Nemo," Kosinski was putting it) was in the habit of showing up nights in the cabin of his, Kosinski's, tiny sailboat, and that it was this Nemo who urged he write the book, going so far as to dictate passages of it and suggest a number of chapter headings. "He sat there looking as real as you or I, Nemo in the old-time Captain's hat that always reminded me of a train conductor punching tickets on the Orient Express. We often had drinks together. Nemo often upbraided me for the cheap wine I was serving. I told him I damned well couldn't afford any but the stuff I got at the discount house."

Whatever the value of that tale, in truth had Kosinski been following through on a boating editor's assignment on the night he was caught peering down Sterling Hayden's kitchen skylight. Kosinski *was* being paid small sums, as had he claimed, for 8 x 10 glossy photographs of what the rich and famous were cooking up in the galleys of their boats and houseboats these days, along with great captions, wouldn't you know, on how to fix the fantastic crap.*

"Having given the bigtime necktie business the old heave-ho, to pursue an existence of love and constant attention to pertinent details of the boating life," Kosinski had written in his odd journal, "I nevertheless found myself in the always peculiar position of having to make a living. That's what they call it, you know. But hear this: I never engage in a line of work that I'm not plumb crazy about so long as I can figure out a way to work around it, ha, ha, ha."

As Alice had told Stanley, it was possible to find a perfectly adequate pair of bolt cutters at any convenient tool rental shop, but none of these would have a Kosinski to rent, not to mention an entire wall rack of possible other adventures. But first they had to find Kosinski, and this was not easy. In fact, "It's like trying to find a haystack in a needle factory," complained Alice after a long day of rowing the dinghy to all the out-of-the-way anchoring places they could think of: a concealed cove here, behind an old pier there, once up a kind of

---

*Shortly after the beef pattie incident, the boating magazine editor fired Kosinski. Said he: "Once he sent us a set of pictures that he claims were of Frankie Laine cooking a pot of spaghetti. It was Frankie Laine, all right, and the boat, that we were able to verify as Laine's sport fisherman down in San Diego. But the pot of spaghetti—Frankie's Mom's Old Favorite: La Forza del Destino & Pasta Suprema, as Kosinski told us it was—hogwash. Kosinski was half a mile away with a borrowed telephoto lens. Laine just happened to be out in the back of the boat washing a rug in a mop pail when Kosinski snapped the pictures.

"We've had to call Tucson, Arizona, no less, to get this tidbit. The man we spoke to has his editorial offices there, in the back of a large, downtown marine supply and recreational vans ('RVs, New and Used') sales outlet. Boating, he told us, has become the rage in Tucson these days, 40- and 50-foot and fully equipped offshore power cruisers being his readers' number one choice. 'Towed behind a Winnebago, along with a couple of snowmobiles and any good off-road vehicle, like a Jeep or rugged Toyota 4 x 4, these boats go to make up quite a rig on the road.'

"Our July cover featured one of these road warriors that measured exactly half a Tucson block long. I paced it off myself and later checked my figures against street department figures for block sizes—and that's the kind of honest boating coverage our readers expect from us. Kosinski made his mistake when he took us for small town fools."

slough that had been hand dug in the 1920s or 30s to give access to the back of a boatbuilder's shed and launch ramp. They found it surprising and frustrating that Kosinski's boat was never to be found where it was said to be on any given day of their getting a fresh new lead from any one of a number of supposedly informed sources. It was as though the boat would magically up and move before ever they were able to get to it.

Kosinski's boat, Alice and Stanley had been told in adequate graphic detail, was easy enough to spot if you knew where to look for it. He had painted it a godawful bright red and given it the name *Da Vinci's Delight*, which he had written in large letters of lime day-glo on a piece of cardboard cut to resemble a ship's life ring, and which was usually to be seen hanging, like a donut, from the tip-end of the bowsprit.

This boat was an 18-foot, gaff-rigged sloop built in 1910 by "an eccentric rich dwarf who below decks modeled the main saloon, such as it was, to look like the ballroom of the Queen Mary. The dwarf and his dwarf girlfriends used to dance up a storm down there, I hear—but I had to sleep on the ballroom floor till I was able to rip out all the dollhouse crap and build a man-sized bunk for myself. Some of the itzy-bitzy furniture the dwarf had had custom built was cute, I guess, but I saved only the pool table. The felt on it was still good, and I used it for a serving tray. Captain Nemo always got a kick out of that. That was one small boat I had, but if you moved around carefully, it was kind of cozy down there. Living on a small boat, ladies and gentlemen, requires a certain flair for developing right attitudes, ha, ha, ha. I felt like a gymnast training for the Olympics in a barrel."

Da Vinci's Delight had no engine. Its mobility was entirely dependent on the set of cotton sails, jib and main (the main had been patched with a portion of blue tablecloth stolen by Kosinski from a restaurant) that had been made as long ago as the boat had. During calms, Kosinski propelled the boat with a 12-foot sweep oar that he set in wooden thole pins mounted on the transom and then sculled, flicking the blade in the water as would a fish its tail.

"It was not a boat easily made to get a move-on pronto, like suddenly in the night," Kosinski has written, "but frequently move it did. I was six months in arrears with the goddamned boat payments.

"When I bought this dumb antique, I put five hundred down. We made a deal that I'd pay such-and-so-much a month. That was fine with me. So I got the boat, and when I got some money from time to time, and if there were any left over after eats and stuff, I'd send the bastards a payment. They were getting a little huffy about this."

It was not entirely his nesting instinct that was driving Kosinski to great ends to outwit the bank loan officer who had taken to prowling the waterfront days and nights at a time to find the boat and, yes, repossess it. Kosinski was busy writing his book *Boat For Broke*, and Captain Nemo, who had appointed himself Kosinski's financial advisor, as we get it, was egging him on with some very irresponsible notions.

"Writing a book takes a lot of thought and careful attention to detail," Kosinski has written. "This didn't leave me a lot of time for much else. Captain Nemo told me not to worry about the bank. 'Do not let them intrude on your existence, sir,' he says. 'Give an inch, they'll take a mile. Already the interest they're charging on this loan of yours is a voracious outrage.' And so nights, in the wee hours when I was down below writing, Captain Nemo would stand watch on the foredeck, always ready to hop-to and man the sculling oar at the first sign of approach.

"So that I could get to the writing first thing, dinners were my usual hearty fare of rice and chopped onions nicely boiled in a sauce of Deaf Smith's natural peanut butter (no goddamned preservatives whatsoever, other than the ones that were keeping me alive) and ketchup, giving me in all much usable protein. I needed this. Writing the book was hard work. The only publisher I could find who was interested in the thing was in Japan. He was the head of the Minimoto Orange Juice & Book Company, with headquarters in Osaka. He was much intrigued that Captain Nemo was the book's technical consultant, as his company had great plans to build a trading submarine of quite advanced design.*

Meantime, the bank loan officer was regularly driving up from his office in Milpitas, about an hour south of Sausalito, in a lavender-pink Cadillac that had in its trunk a 20-foot length of chain and a heavy-duty brass padlock. The banker's technique, Kosinski had learned from deadbeat boat owner friends of his who were also in arrears, was the customary one of first finding the boat's location and then hiring a local informer (always one with a fast boat for hire) to keep a watch on it. Then, when it had been determined by observation that Kosinski, say, was to be away from the boat for any time (was he seen to pack a bag, catch a bus for out-of-town, say?)—Lo, the informer would call the bank collect, the banker would come pronto with the chain and lock. The two would speed out to the target's place of anchorage, tow it off to a secret location and there chain it to the dock.

As was the procedure in any instance, Kosinski would later

---

*Sir Anton Ritter-LaRue, in his chapter entitled (liberally, we quote the whole thing) Will the Real Captain Nemo Please Bob Up, If Still He Inhabits the Ocean, His Adopted Country, would seem to give substance to what here appears a mere curiosity.

"More so than the French," he would have us know, "are the Japanese dangerously close to being gaga in their energetic enthusiasm for 'Captain Nemo-san, neo-samuri of the sea with his submersible technological solutions to a new world order,' and so they put it, there in this portion of the indeed mysterious East. Here, Wu's wee Lu Pan is seen as a cheap, Chinese trinket without finesse. To the modern Japanese mind, Wu altogether missed the boat.

"Coded into the book Twenty Thousand Leagues Under the Sea were indeed such features of anticipatory design in undersea vessels as would be understood only in Japan, where principles of design and myth are regularly joined—and, eventually, produced. But it is the Japanese feeling that only Captain Nemo himself knew the particulars of Jules Verne's at once broad strokes and coded messages. It was as though Verne was giving out blueprints whose fine details came to light only if one knew to steam these over some boiling orange juice concoction, or such."

Unfortunately, Sir Anton leaves out in his concoction the Western notion of Captain Nemo (-san or otherwise) as "the romantic exile, the misunderstood Byronic hero fighting for Greek independence." The words are Walter James Miller's. Nor does he mention that in Japan are the Nemo gaga-san, with government backing, producing quite a series of yet-to-be-released sci-fi flicks, in the most exquisite color you ever saw. The Minimoto Orange Juice & Book Company had joined the government in backing the production of these films. Moshiro Tofuni stars and directs.

find in his post office box notice that his personal possessions—
clothes, books, typewriter, tools, manuscript, foodstuffs, and
all—were in boxes at the bank in Milpitas, and that *Da Vinci's
Delight* was being put up for auction. He would be invited to
pick up his personal possessions at any time during specified
bank hours, and he would be told he could have his boat back if
he could come up with the full balance owing before a given
date of public auction. The bank, then, without the due process
afforded the home buyer, say, would have achieved unmessy
eviction of the tenant and the repossession of his aquatic
dwelling in one fell swoop.

First thing when he heard about this procedure, and after
getting from a maritime attorney verification of the regular
application of it by vexed boat loan vendors generally,
Kosinski, quick, told his pal Captain Nemo the whole story.
Nemo, then, says Kosinski, got mad and fired off a telegram to
the bank in Milpitas. "Catch Kosinski as catch can," this said.
"*Mobilis in Mobili*, or, quote, always on the move as befits these
perilous times. Do not intrude on my existence, gentlemen.
Kosinski's floating house and home is not yours to repossess,
ha, ha, ha." The telegram was boldly signed, "Captain Nemo,
Commander of the Submarine *Nautilus*, Pilot in Residence, *Da
Vinci's Delight*." The bank, it appears, got irate. But to achieve
any sense of completion in what it was irate about, first the
loan officer had to find Kosinski's boat, and of course were his
efforts stepped up. Being nothing less than the great naval
tactician he was, says Kosinski, Captain Nemo knew to
anticipate the banker's every move. Still—and against a fear
that worse could come to worst—Kosinski bought a pair of the
best used chain and bolt cutters he could find and afford. He
took to sleeping with these wrapped in a blanket under his
pillow.

During this difficult period, was it, that Kosinski was having
bad dreams—spectral dreams. Was he regretting his impulsive, spectral pursuit of the boating life? It is best, however,
that Kosinski tell us about this his way:

When I quit the bigtime gaudy necktie business to take up the
boating life, L. Gordon Strong, the big cheese upstairs, said, 'If I

followed your advice and one by one shoved up my ass all the
hand-painted silk neckties this company has had made in
Taiwan and Cairo these past twenty-five years—that's a lot of
neckties, Kosinski—I would be ahead of the game and you
would be the loser. Quit now and go boating, and everything
you've worked for all these years goes down the drain.'

'If I have to go down the drain to get out of this dreary racket,'
I told L. Gordon Strong—'show me where it is.' All drains, if they
don't have their plumbing screwed up, lead eventually to the
sea.

So now, asleep in my bunk nights, I dream of the banker after
my ass. The neckties czar haunts my worst dreams, his gaudy
Egyptian necktie aflap in the spectral wind as he shouts at me
through a cheap, tin horn, 'Go to hell—you're finished,
Kosinski!'

My so-far 2,000-page book has forever to go until it is
finished. The publishers here in this country think I'm crazy, ha,
ha, ha. One of 'em writes to me and says he doesn't think the
reading public is ready for 'such a work of personal honesty as
claims to have been dictated in large part by *the* Captain Nemo,
as you say. Tut, tut, Mr. Kosinski. What today's reader demands
is knowledge of how to make, in no more than six easy steps, an
inexpensive foldaway coffee table for his weekend putt-putt
boat. Little nuts and bolts, Mr. Kosinski—not your two-
thousand-and-some pages of sordid boating tales and crackpot
how-to advice cooked up by you and this phantom friend of
yours.'

The man of Osaka, the sole publisher interested in this
fascinating work these days, thinks I have only a few more
chapters to go before revealing the complete plans to Captain
Nemo's old submarine so that they can take them down to the
Honda factory and have them build it. Well, with all this,
wouldn't you know, Kosinski is flat broke and in deep, hot
water.

But I say it twice, I say it three times, ladies and gentlemen:
Ha, ha, ha. Boiled Bermuda onions, when I can get 'em fresh
from the flea market, and Deaf Smith's all-natural peanut butter
(pretty damned crunchy, that stuff) have made of Smasden
Kosinski a pretty tough nut, I tell you. *Nemo dat quod non
habet*—or as it is spoken in the certainly more familiar
vernacular, 'No man can give what he does not have.' Need I go
on?

Whether he needs to or not is beside the point, Kosinski *does*
go on. In both his better and his worst passages he likens
himself to "a frequently drunk monk in a boat with cupboards

bare, cloistered next the bushy berm and covered all over with burlap sacks and raspberry vines, while with red, felt-tipped marking pen I coin, a penny at a time (how I long for the sharp edge of a crisp, green ten-spot), these aquatic beatitudes of mine of shimmering heartfelt crimson. . . ."

Good heavens, Kosinski. We are red with embarrassment.

What he is trying to tell us is that he was during the days hiding out in a tiny cove once favored by bootleggers for its junglelike concentration of tan oaks, poplars, cattails, willows, and tall bamboos—as though the booze smugglers had from 1920 through 1933 seeded the place with every variety of screening vegetation they could get their hands on. No wonder Stanley and Alice were taking so long to find Kosinski. The banker, fortunately, was to have an even more difficult time of it. Not only was Kosinski successfully taking advantage of the cove's dense and natural bower—he had covered the boat all over with burlap sacks and raspberry vines cut from along the old railroad track on shore.

If *Boat For Broke* had grown to 2,000 and more pages, it wasn't because he was writing that much. He was using bold strokes of nontoxic red marker to scribe his stuff on page after page of old newspapers. His preference was for the want ad sections, their lack of obtrusive headlines and their dull small type giving excellent contrast to the thick, red lines of his boating thoughts—"his aquatic beatitudes and his aquatic attitudes." Well, now.

"Wait till the man from Osaka reads this, ha, ha, ha," he would sometimes say to himself in an aside to the mainstream of his thought, and then feverishly would he write ten or twenty pages describing various intimate features of Nemo's old submarine, illuminating these with what he said were precise drawings of this or that technical detail. These he would bundle up with string and have sent to Osaka, by way of an arrangement with the Japanese trade center in San Francisco. He had only to phone and recite a code phrase ("Captain Nemo lives"), and then they would send a courier.

Kosinski would meet the courier in the back of an alley or behind a designated building in a deserted section of the industrial section of Sausalito. The Japanese was always well dressed, as if high-placed in an important government agency.

He spoke English not too badly, Kosinski tells us, and was formal in the old way. Handing over the packet, Kosinski would bow deeply and say, "Do we not seek departure from instruction altogether, that we might invent and reinvent the nature of our existence, ha, ha, ha? Here are the plans."

The Japanese would return Kosinski's bow, if in a deeper and more practiced way, and say, "As we say in Japan, Kosinski-san, what is right cannot for long be wrong, provided one puts one's mind to it. Kudasai—for the plans." He would take Kosinski-san's roll of newsprint tied with string and go, till next time.

The bulk of *Boat for Broke*, with its private musings, potty poems, screwball boating advice, and scurrilous, scrimshaw tales—this Kosinski-san kept for himself, in behalf of future posterity at home, he liked to think.

It was just after one of the meetings between the Mikado and the Münchausen that Alice was about to round the corner of a deserted building in the old industrial district, on the advice of a supposedly informed source who knew positively that Kosinski was living in the back of a deserted upholstery shop a few doors from there. The information was misperceived, to be sure, but did produce surprising results. The regular afternoon wind, trumpeting, as always it did, the arrival of clouds of sea fog in the ridges of the hills above town, whipped around the corner of the building as Alice thrust a foot beyond its shadow in preparation of swinging a sharp left.

At that same instant, galloping toward her along the ground, came a hat that made a kind of clopping noise each time the wind rolled it full cycle. The hard, black bill of the hat would come round and strike the pavement, leaving in its track a comet tail of bits of sand and small particles of road gravel.

Chasing after it came Kosinski, who, as abruptly as had the hat, rounded the corner at the building's opposite end, the hat having rolled the length of the short alley fronting the building. But abruptly again, Kosinski braked with the heels of both Keds when he saw Alice. She was holding the hat before her with both hands, turning it this way and that and peering at it intently.

What she found herself holding was one of those old-time

sea captain's hats that disappointingly look a lot like the unfashionable sort of drumhead jobs worn by ticket punchers on trains. Scraps and pieces of paper, hastily scribbled notes obviously, were here and there poking out of the black leather band that lined the inside of the hat's brim.

In all, this antique hat of questionable nineteenth century aquatic conceit was just as Captain Ernie had described it—a Captain Nemo hat of the sort that some kook might wear while operating a homemade diving bell that was momentarily tangled in kelp off the coast of Madagascar. Alice felt confident in supposing that the bare head of the man staring at her from around the building's opposite corner was that of the hat's rightful and apparently ruffled owner.

"I've heard so much about you," she said. "It is Mr. Kosinski, I presume."

Kosinski looked her up and down, rubbing wind-ruffled, white hairs with a white-gloved hand. Instinctively, he had withdrawn from sight most of the map of his face, so that what peered at Alice from around the building's stucco corner was but one, very wide-open eye.

"It depends who's asking," said Kosinski. "Give me back the hat."

"Captain Ernie suggested we look you up if we needed help in a difficult boating matter," said Alice. "This is some antique, this hat. Is it authentic?"

"I didn't get it out of some rent-by-the-day costume shop and then forget to bring it back," said Kosinski. "I beat Captain Nemo out of it in a game of Battleship. He was a little tight that night. He's not used to these cheap, brandy-spiked California sherries I get at the discount store. So you're a friend of Captain Ernie's, eh?"

Alice made to throw the hat to Kosinski. A hand of his reached out from the building to catch it. But she had to stop and think a moment. Kosinski saw the look of consternation cross her face.

"It was a fair game," he said. "I sank all his subs, and then a heavy cruiser. He had no choice."

"That wasn't what I was thinking," said Alice. "You two really did play Battleship—toy battleships and, my God, toy subs?

"Really what I'm thinking, Mr. Kosinski, if that's who you are, is would Lord Nelson at home play with bathtub toy squareriggers in anticipation of the Battle of Trafalgar? Would Neptune not sneer at the suggestion of a game of water polo with a lot of silly school girls cavorting naked in the surf?

"Oh, hell," Alice corrected herself, "he probably would go for it. I got myself screwed up with that last messy metaphor."

"What the hell do I care what a sailor does on his time off?" shouted Kosinski. "If he knits, ties knots, shoots craps, crochets doilies out of saltwater taffy—that's his damned business. Give me back my hat."

"Well," said Alice, "when you put it that way, then I have to say that any friend of Captain Nemo's is a friend of mine. Here's your hat. Catch. . . ."

Alice threw the hat. Kosinski, a hand darting out from the wall, caught it on the fly. He put in on his head and patted it down to a good, tight fit. He stepped out from behind the building, bowed, and clicked his heels. "Likewise, I'm sure," he said. "Any friend of Captain Ernie's is a friend of Smasden Kosinski's."

"Then it is you," said Alice. "I'm delighted. But wouldn't you know. I almost forgot what I came for."

"What's that?" said Kosinski.

"Bolt cutters," said Alice. "I'm in a bit of a jam myself. . . ."

Chapter *15*

Breaking Away

Potent Quotes

"Thus ends the voyage under the seas. What passed during the night—how the boat escaped from the eddies of the maelstrom . . . I cannot tell.

But when I returned to consciousness, I was lying in a fisherman's hut, on the Loffoden Isles. My two companions, safe and sound, were near me holding hands. We embraced each other heartily.

But whatever became of the Nautilus? Does Captain Nemo still live?

I hope so."

Jules Verne

"The Loffoden Islands, huh. So where the hell's that?"

Smasden Kosinski

$\mathcal{OS}$ MASDEN KOSINSKI-SAN'S INVOLVEMENT WITH the Minimoto Orange Juice & Book Company's odd plans to build a submarine that is superior to Captain Nemo's charming but antique one—well, this would seem to go to make a fine and far-out pot of bouillabaisse and a new genre of boating tale, perhaps. Would we need to call this concoction Boating Science Fiction?

Kosinski, in the introduction to his book (and here we are, coming to the end of this one) says there is every indication that the American boating public is ready for this. "We live in a science fiction world these days that requires science fiction solutions to even boating. We need to acquire the means and right attitudes that will allow us to boat-for-broke with the best of them. Hear, hear. Avast (hold fast), and on with it!"*

Our subject of timely critical interest in this present book, however, is a pair of good, old-fashioned bolt cutters, plus the chain of events following Alice's chance meeting with Kosinski. Will Kosinski be so kind as to loan his out to a perfect stranger? Or will he feel a desperate need to hang on to these, "just in case"?

A tall, thin banker with eyes like the wetted cotton ends of swab sticks is several times a week driving up from Milpitas to look for Kosinski, padlock and chain kept in a steely coil in the

---

*In the conclusion to his book (which only a publisher in Hong Kong would issue, by the way, and then as an adjunct to the firm's booming business in Chinese navigational instruments and sailing charts), Sir Anton Ritter-LaRue makes an interesting point. He perceives the entire world population as being boaters, "a vast republic, if you will, from birth to death forever adrift on these great, clanking, stone boats we call continents. No wonder that this great captive boating public should crave boating books more realistic than the ones they're getting from some publishers we can name."

As long as we're on this business of book endings (the best of which always are great beginnings to something better than the book itself), we might just as well pass on what Jules Verne says at the tag-end of his Captain Nemo tale. "Does Captain Nemo still live? And does he follow under the ocean those frightful retaliations?" And then, after suggesting the possibility, he says, "If Captain Nemo still inhabits the ocean, his adopted country... if his destiny be strange, it is also sublime." We, for one, would be the last to find fault with this conclusion.

trunk of the lavender-pink Cadillac. And what Kosinski doesn't know is that more recently has the banker hired an accomplice—a cop (more bad bread upon the waters?) with instructions to keep an eye peeled when during an occasional off-duty hour or so (the bank is picking up his gas tab, in addition to offering a finder's fee) he putts and prowls in his 18-foot launch with its folding canvas top and surprising capacity to sleep four in comfort over a holiday weekend, say. As a matter of fact, the cop during his patrols is taking along two young women—a couple of gorgeous go-go dancers who during *their* off-duty hours like to drop anchor and go for it, in tandem with the cop, and then lie around afterwards tanning in the sun. Combining, as he does, boating business with boating pleasure this way, the cop may be a while before finding Kosinski.

The problem is (if this *is* the problem), there are others who are after Kosinski, too. When he quit the necktie business, told the boss to go to hell and all, Kosinski emptied his display case of handpainted Oriental neckties up and down Howard Street—gave one free to any one of the down-and-out, deadbeat, wine-sodden regulars of that dark neighborhood who would have one. Overnight, gray, grim Howard Street burst into a flame of walking, shuffling, gaudy, tropical splendor. L. Gordon Strong got himself punched in the face trying to reclaim at least one of his precious ties. No dice. He went to small claims court, sued and won, and now a sheriff's man is after Kosinski's belated payment of $925 and some few cents.

Kosinski's former wife, who runs a kids' dance studio in downtown Milpitas (suburban brats in tutus, folding chairs oozing with droppings of bean burritos and Slurpees dragged in from the 7–11 next door), has been months now vowing she would kill Kosinski. Her new boy friend, the town fire marshall, is getting the district attorney to indict Kosinski for arson. Did not Kosinski, on the night after maliciously trashing valuable merchandise owned by a certain purveyor of neckties, return home in a state of intoxication and set fire to the lawn in front of the house by pouring on it a dangerously combustible substance obtained from the fuel tank of his wife's power lawnmower? Did not the aforementioned drunken loon, moments before his admitted flight from, in his words, these stinking little lawns and empty patches of suburban nothing, cry out, so that his neighbors up and down the block called the police to report an earthquake and hazardous fire, "Fuck this place. Kosinski's headed for the bosom of the sea, pronto!— Captain Nemo still lives. It's the goddamn suburbs that are dead"?

Yes, yes, Kosinski was guilty of all this crime against sleeping suburban humanity. He wanted out. He went. And now they were after him. "Really, now," Captain Nemo was advising him at this critical juncture, Kosinski has written, "there's no harm in loaning out the bolt cutters. In fact, you might as well give them away. The pickle you're in—I would say that extraordinary measures are in order."

Captain Nemo had made one of his rare daytime appearances, which, when these did occur, Kosinski came to associate with an unusually high morning tide brought on by the lunar phase known as the new moon. It was also a time when Kosinski felt unnaturally agitated and was having the worst kind of bad dreams.

"Any ideas?" asked Kosinski. He made to pour the Captain a glass of wine, but Nemo, sitting back in the starboard bunk of *Da Vinci's Delight*'s tiny main saloon, stayed him with a wave of the hand. "How many times do I have to tell you, Kosinski," he said, "—my cook is a very clever fellow. You are not so fraught with these troubles of yours that you don't get my meaning, I hope."

"Well, I've never seen him cook up anything around here that was any great shakes," said Kosinski. "Maybe it is because my pantry is as bare as the good Captain's head these days."

Captain Nemo scratched the top of his head with noticeable irritation. "Watch what you say," he said. "There's more here than meets the eye. And there's more in this pantry of *mine* than even poor Jules knew to write about. He didn't know the half of it."

"You don't say," said Kosinski.

"I do," said Captain Nemo. "If you'll give me back my hat for an instant. All right, *your* hat. It has certain powers, if you know how to use it. Right now, I want to make a quick check of my cook's menu. The hat is far better than any computer in that respect. It puts me in touch with a greater selection of hot and spicy possibilities. The hat, Mr. Kosinski."

Kosinski removed the hat from his head and gave it to Captain Nemo to wear for the time. And Captain Nemo, adjusting the hat on his head with the care he might have given to touch-tuning any good, ship's radio direction finder, closed his eyes in deep thought and concentration, and said, "We're all in the same boat, we are. We have to stick together."

"What boat?" said Kosinski.

"We who boat-for-broke. We boat people," said Captain Nemo. "That's the boat we're in. Now, then, silence, Kosinski. No more talk. I'm envisioning a meaty solution to what ails a few of us here."

He leaned back in the bunk, closed both eyes, stuck a finger in each of his ears, puffed up his cheeks as if in preparation of blowing out birthday candles on a cake two miles away. The top of his hat began to emit dancing blue sparks. But suddenly his cheeks went flat, he pulled his fingers out of his ears, the little blue sparks vanished.

"There is just one more thing before we get on with this," said Captain Nemo. "I want to make this quite clear, Kosinski.

"It is personalities and not principles that govern the universe. Oscar Wilde said that, but he got it from me. He did not quote me altogether accurately. In his efforts to be the succinct smart-ass, he did not add, as I do now, that the truth of what I said applies not only to the universe but everything in it. This is especially true of whatsoever it is that has anything at all to do with boats."

"I know," said Kosinski. "Give some people a boat, and they think they own the world."

"Conversely," said Captain Nemo, "give some people a little authority in this world, and they extend this in the name of principle to include the very last threshold of freedom on earth."

"Right," said Kosinski, "—boats."

"Precisely," said Captain Nemo. "I had every reason to suppose you knew this, Kosinski. I merely wanted to be sure we had accord on this before doing what must be done."

"Unusual situations do require unusual measures. Let fly," said Kosinski.

Again, Captain Nemo squinched shut his eyes, put a finger in each ear, puffed his cheeks. The little blue sparks coming from his hat made Kosinski's eyes water and burn. The noise these made, which was like that of static blasting from a powerful radio transmitter not quite tuned to the proper frequency, made the insides of Kosinski's ears clack and rattle. Toward the end, a long, white spark grew from the end of his nose and then exploded with a thunder clap that filled his nostrils with the pungent smell of scorched ozone.

"I felt I was being drawn through an overheated wire filled with banging, colliding electrons rushing to catch a nonstop flight to Japan. For a moment I was lost in trying to find from which concourse the flight was departing.

"As I, too, plugged my fingers with my ears," Kosinski has written, "I had every reason to have faith that a great result would follow from this experiment, with good news for all." In his book, *Boat For Broke*, there are no "surprise" clauses to keep us glued to our seats in breezy anticipation of predictable results. In this book, we just tell it like it is and quickly get on with the "what happened next" part. What happened next was this:

Well, not more than 72 hours had passed since her meeting with Captain-Fellow Kosinski-san, and it was obvious now that the guy had connections. Alice was neither awake nor asleep but caught in a dozy-delirium in which waiting for the ship's clock to ring soft chimes tolling midnight became a matter of demonically rearranging, over and over again, the placement of rugs and furniture on the ocean bottom, all of it refusing to stay put for long and turning slow spirals on its way to rising to the surface.

Minutes and seconds of time became as rocks placed on rug corners and on the seats of couches and chairs, and still would the stuff not stay put. Alice was mad at her mind for insisting she be kept half awake to measure the passage of time in this fashion. But while fussing and fidgeting, the spectral house-keeping never to be done to lasting and final satisfaction, she consoled herself with the thought that these were unusual times, all right, and that therefore had time to be unusual too. It was just then that the clock tolled midnight. She became brightly awake and alert to odd sounds that were enveloping the *Lu Pan* in a kind of sentient mist, she likened it to be, that began with a pleasant snip-snap and an almost inaudible splash of a 12-foot length of chain being deftly and delicately cast into the waters, ha, ha, ha.

"There's no need to bother Stanley with the details," she had been told. "This would only spoil a great surprise and lessen the sense of mystery of it all." And so she let Stanley sleep his sleep of rapid eye movements as he lay curled next to her under the quilt.

The flicking of his eyes this way and that under tightly closed lids were those of the dreamer watching the video events of his dream, and Stanley was dreaming that he was Captain Nemo, Alice Mrs. Nemo, that they were hard at work on a deserted beach seeking to produce a Little Nemo.

Whether the beach was a Hawaiian, a Micronesian, or a far more distant one, he couldn't be sure. He didn't look to see, as the rapid movements of his eyes were locked in on the up-and-down wiggles and jiggles as Alice's breasts went in syncopation to the thrusts of ecstatic hip and pelvic muscles. He liked having Alice on top and in this dream the view and its ancillary sensations were splendid. Alice, from her vantage point, enjoyed the perception of still other anatomical events of their making at this moment, and she, too, was having rapid eye movements. Thus his dream was complete in its satisfactions, and he was content to continue having it.

As had been suggested to Alice, likely not another person asleep on a boat there in Marina Regalis Estate's small harbor would be jarred out of sleep by those stealthily at work that night. At one point, she heard a sort of gliding, sliding, thunking noise coming from the vicinity of the *Lu Pan*'s cockpit. But this failed to stir even Stanley. Did she at the time smell the smell of scorched, stale chicken grease? She was quite sure she had. Commander-Harbormaster Push-Pin Renfrow, she supposed, had for some reason not removed the chicken half from the hibachi's grill, and now the whole works was being conscientiously returned.

She heard and felt the *Lu Pan*'s docklines being slipped and then stowed on deck (she heard the lines being laid in no doubt neat coils), and it was just then that she felt Stanley begin to nudge her with the hardness that had been fashioned in his video dreamland. He was likely to awaken and start to paw, she knew from experience, and so she reached under the quilt and grasped him in hand, thinking as she did so that the situation was likely to get stickier than she had imagined. But if this kept the sleeper happy in his dreams, as indeed his autoharp bumps and grinds indicated, she at least wouldn't have *that* messing up things.

In any event, thought Alice, this was certainly in keeping with the advice of hours ago, to just let things happen naturally, and then it would all come out to a good end. And now she felt the *Lu Pan* being slowly pulled out of its slip. The black-gloved hands of experts were at work handing a towline, working it in foot by foot so as to quietly swing 'round the boat and get it on its way out the harbor entrance and into the bay beyond.

Cousins of these hands, similarly gloved in black silk, had worked their way into the basement apartment on Chestnut Street, in San Francisco, where the sprouting avocado seeds sat in the kitchen window. Shogun-Admiral Hop-A-Long Snit Foot, snoring soundly in his bed of mawpy-mandate dreams (fee/fines for the world, a blistering attack of paper and writs), did not feel the covers lift, and neither did his snoring wife feel nor hear anything. He did not feel the joss sticks and the firecrackers being inserted in the spaces between each of his ten toes. Shouldn't these be put in each of his ears, up his nose, too, it was argued in cautious whispers.

But, no, it was thrashed out in whispers more sonorous but every bit as cautious—this is not the way of the Ninja Branch of the Captain Nemo Fan Club of Japan, nor the way of the club's corporate sponsors who provided the members their uniforms of black felt sneakers, baggy Kung-Fu pants and matching jackets with hoods. The big plus of this sponsorship was the annual pilgrimage—the Minimoto Orange Juice & Book Company offering cut-rate air fare to those in good standing—to Amiens, France, where the devotees gathered at Jules Verne's graveside to eat chicken teriyaki provided in Bento box lunches, drink sake, and chant prayers whose incantations, in Japanese, were taken from the words Jules Verne had himself inscribed on his tombstone: "Onward to Immortality and Eternal Youth." And so these chants and incantations went, until late in the summer night the styrofoam Bento boxes and the bottles and bottles of sake emptied to nothing.

No, it was not the way of these small men dressed all in black to blow up Commandant Fuss-Fool's toes, possibly his wife's too, and likely set his apartment on fire. This was not their cup of crude tea. In the snorey darkness of the basement apartment, fuses were lighted, scented punk sticks set to burning. And then, just before the firecrackers banged—strings and packets of the delicate but chain-reaction Lady Fingers dangling from the two- and three-inch Hong Kong Bombers laced between his toes—fuses were snuffed, punk sticks squelched: he would wake up in the morning to the fright of what might have been had less subtle souls been there to visit that night.

As it was, when he did wake up that morning, his eyes would grow as big as balloons as with trembling fingers ("Look sharp," he would caution himself, "—one of these could go off any second") he one by one removed the Hong Kong Bombers and their wriggly packets of lesser crackers, each with its scorched, pinched-off-at-the-last-minute fuse suggesting a condition of critical instability. "They didn't train you for this in the Navy," his wife would shout. "Use your head. Call the bomb squad."

"For chrissake, shut up," he would shout back, "—you're making the bed shake."

Later, in the kitchen and by the coffee maker, he would find the departed gentlemen's calling card, along with several attractive four-color brochures showing a nice variety of

Minimoto Orange Juice & Book Company products, including
their latest "Ready-When-The-Coffee-Is" automatic orange
juice maker. The calling card accompanying this presentation
was printed in the likeness of a small orange folded down the
center to give the appearance of being but half of one. When
you opened out the card, as Renfrow did—presto, it became the
whole orange. Holding the card toward you as you opened it,
out would spring a paper chain of little men all in black, doll-
like cutouts done in the delicate origami fashion, that bounced
and jiggled in perfect unison if you shook the card, as did
Renfrow, out of sheer curiosity.

But what most caught the eye of Dominus-vobiscum Would-
be Soot Foot was the calling card's handwritten note. "Boat
people," it said, "—you're messing around with the wrong
bunch. Any more of this, we'll have your hide. So, pal, what
you better do is keep on your toes from here on in, ha, ha,
ha.

"*Mobilis in Mobili*, Toot, Toot, and All Around, and as Captain
Nemo says, My Cook Is a Clever Fellow—you just better believe
it."

Well, from that time on, down at the docks at Marina Regalis
Estates they called him Right-on Renfrow, one of the most
pleasant and helpful of harbormasters that ever hopped right
over to help out a boater. Rather than hand out mawpy
mandates, writs, and fee/fines, he got into the habit of handing
out boxes of candy, gift certificates to his and the Missus'
favorite discount store, Bible tracts and prayer cards, and a
printed message of his own addressed "To Christian Boating
Couples With Kids." The card's message was short. It said, "Tell
the children to be good little boys and girls—or the little men
in black will come in the night and stick firecrackers in your
toes." As some of the guests at Marina Regalis Estates began to
suspect, Right-on Renfrow had gone a bit potty. Also from that
time on was he sleeping with his socks on, thick, white wool
ones with the tops fastened down by stainless steel bicycle
clips.

Next to his bed he kept a shotgun. As he told his wife, "If the
sons of bitches show their faces again, they're in for a big
surprise."

"Well, if you're Napoleon," said his wife, "I'm Josephine—and I should think now we can afford one of those new automatic orange juice makers. It takes half the day to squeeze juice with the one we have, and the rest of the day to clean the thing."

"Damn the Minimoto orange juice maker," shouted Renfrow. "Cheap, Oriental junk." He reached out, banged the butt of the shotgun on the bedroom floor. It went off, BOOM. The upstairs neighbors raised quite a stink about that. Well, to put it in the writing business vernacular, that wraps up Renfrow. But our story does not end here of course.

There's nothing like a good breakfast to get a hard day's boating activity off on the right foot, and Stanley, certainly, was desperate to have his. "I suppose all this is your idea," he said to Alice. "Yours and this Kosinski character's." He had slept soundly and dreamt well enough all the while the *Lu Pan* was being towed out to sea. Alice, the munchy muse of his dream of a previous predawn hour, had sat in the cockpit steering. Now, with the sun of honest dawn illuminating the thick, white fog all around, he was able to see that they weren't in indisputable fact at sea but just then passing under the Golden Gate Bridge. It was here that the sea began and San Francisco Bay left off. A heady transition zone, this, where escaping bay waters clashed with incoming sea swells in narrow straits not designed for two-way traffic of this kind during the tidal rush hour.

"If the tow line holds, we'll make it," said Alice. "If it breaks, there's not much use hauling up sail. The only wind we've got is the one we're making."

"Right," said Stanley, who was rummaging one of the cockpit storage lockers looking for the coffee can full of charcoal tinder of bits of dried sticks, wood shavings, and sawdust, all of it soaked in kerosene, that always he used to fire up the hibachi.

"What have we got to eat?" he said. "We really ought to have stopped at the store before getting underway like this. There isn't another Safeway for the next 2,000 miles, I hear."

"Honolulu is more like 2,200 miles, I think," said Alice. "But they promised that before they cast us off they'll give us all the supplies we need, including oranges and one of their no-nonsense juicers that you work by hand. It's the model that sells so well all over the South Pacific where people don't have Pacific Gas & Electric to plug into."

"It had damned well better work," said Stanley. "Anything I hate, it's a dumb-shit orange juice maker that takes all day and twenty oranges to make a glass."

"I think this one will surprise you," said Alice. "These people are clever. They've redesigned the whole concept. But all there is for breakfast just now is a canned whole chicken I've been saving. It's the one we got in Chinatown last year."

"Jesus holy smuckers," shouted Stanley. "The only thing anyone ever eats in this book is chicken—and now the only one we've got is a canned one bought in July and here it is March. It's going to taste like warmed-over tin."

"It's all we got," said Alice. "It's precooked. All you have to do is heat it a little. Maybe make a sauce when we get out of this slop and you can put the wok on the hibachi without everything spilling out of it."

"I'm hungry as hell," said Stanley. "We'll eat it out of the can."

Just then was the *Lu Pan* sucked into the trough of a steep wave broiling by like river rapids. Like an elevator whose cable had slipped, the *Lu Pan* dropped two floors. Stanley just in time pulled away his hand as the lid of the locker he was rummaging slammed shut and burst its hinges. The boat lurched and shuddered as the thick towline pulled the boat by its bow out of the trough and then over and through the wave's steep, breaking top. Another of these strange waves awaited them on the other side.

"Time-warp time," said Alice. She braced both feet against the cockpit floor. Both hands grasped the bucking tiller. "What—another ten minutes before we're out of this stuff?"

Stanley eyed the towline. It was stretched as taut as a giant rubber band. "I'd still like to know just who the hell is pulling us along out here," he said. The towline was perfectly visible for forty or fifty yards, and then gradually, like the centerline of a road rushing beyond the range of speeding headlights, vanished into a vaporous wall of blazing, white fog.

Stanley peered over the *Lu Pan*'s side. He was fascinated by the crazed and crazy currents that in this zone of transition from the landed and the littoral to the expansive and the oceanic ran every which way, in accordance with forces not visible to the eye. The trough they'd just been hauled through, and now the similarly goofy canyonland they'd just plunged into, these he recognized the instant as being in part, at least, the production staged by Pacific Ocean swells when under the Golden Gate they met head-on gurgling surges of bay tide thick with gathered soil runoff and bottom muds, bits of boards and trees, sudsy sewer effluent that was like tapioca made bubbly with bursts of methane gas, lost shoes and socks (never in matched pairs), partially deflated tire tubes, bottles, condoms, milk cartons, cardboard boxes, torn bits of black and white plastic sheeting, and God knows what. Yes, another ten minutes of slogging through this stuff before they would encounter the ocean swells born pure and simple thousands of miles to seaward and herded toward the land by massive winds whose shouts and hoots were to be heard miles and eons beyond and over the Western ocean horizon.

Now, advancing toward the *Lu Pan*'s port side, also being hauled along by a tow line but strangely, as was the wish of these currents here, sliding along sideways even as it was pulled forward, came through fragments and wisps of thick and thin white fog Smasden Kosinski's *Da Vinci's Delight*. "Ahoy, *Lu Pan*," shouted Kosinski through a megaphone as rapidly the distance between the two boats began to close.

"Hi," said Alice.

"The crazy sonofabitch is going to hit us," said Stanley.

"Like I said, ha, ha, ha," shouted Kosinski. "What the hell we hanging around yacht harbors and marinas for when there's a whole big world out here." He stood in the cockpit wearing his Captain Nemo's hat and hanging onto the forestay with one hand as the boat plunged and skidded through the same stuff that the *Lu Pan* traveled with much the same difficulty.

"Anything for breakfast?" he shouted. "I'm famished."

"Don't come near," shouted Stanley. "We'll smash to bits."

But as the situation would have it, just then did the towlines of both boats get up just a bit more speed, for now were they

out of the slop and into that other zone of so-far quiet, each
ocean roller rising and falling with rhythms that seemed those
of a whale breathing in sleep. But again was Kosinski's boat
slipping sideways, this time away from the *Lu Pan* and back
into the concealing fog.

"See you later," shouted Kosinski. "Once out of this fog,
they'll cast us loose and we're on our own, ha, ha, ha. *Mobilis in
Mobili*, my friends. We are called into the Pacific on a far greater
journey, no? Well, in any event, the bosoms of the sea are big
enough for us all, I hope." And then did he completely vanish
in the fog.

"Gee," said Alice, "I'm beginning to worry will we ever see
him again. Did you notice?"

"What, that his rudder was gone?" said Stanley. "Not only
that, his boat was really low in the water. Does he have a
leak?"

"Probably," said Alice. "Don't worry. He'll figure out
something."

"Maybe so," said Stanley. "He's got that look about him."

Well, there they go. Not off into the sunset, exactly. But off,
anyway. Alice and Stanley, we know, will get to Hawaii and
then go off to Majuro, where first we met them in this book of
strange currents under the bridge. As for Smasden Kosinski-
san and his Minimoto Orange Juice & Book Company pals—
that stuff is not within the scope of our current reportage. It is
just too much to fit in, frankly.

At the end of his book of boat tales, Sir Anton Ritter-LaRue
concludes, "After looking it all over, from truck to keelson and
sideways (and you do have to look sideways), one is compelled
to say it just makes you want to go out and buy one—buy a
boat, that is, and just go for it."

Now, at the conclusion of this book, we have to say that his is
not so much sound advice as it is a way of looking at things. It
seems a safe conclusion, then—and without being so cautious
as to not say it at all—that this is one of those things you have
to decide for yourself. Some people don't like chicken, no
matter how it's fixed, for example, and some do, again, no
matter how it's fixed. You can say the same about boats, I
would think, and not go too far wrong.